Great Pajama
Jobs

Great Pajama Jobs

Your Complete Guide to Working from Home

By Kerry Hannon

Best-selling Author, *The New York Times* Columnist,
Career Expert

WILEY

Library of Congress Cataloging-in-Publication Data:

Names: Hannon, Kerry, author.
Title: Great pajama jobs : your complete guide to working from home / by Kerry
    Hannon, Best-selling author, The New York Times columnist, career expert.
Description: First edition. | Hoboken, New Jersey : Wiley, [2020] |
    Includes index.
Identifiers: LCCN 2020019781 (print) | LCCN 2020019782 (ebook) | ISBN
    9781119647775 (paperback) | ISBN 9781119647782 (Adobe PDF) | ISBN
    9781119647751 (epub)
Subjects: LCSH: Telecommuting. | Job hunting. | Work environment.
Classification: LCC HD2336.3 .H36 2020 (print) | LCC HD2336.3 (ebook) |
    DDC 650.14—dc23
LC record available at https://lccn.loc.gov/2020019781
LC ebook record available at https://lccn.loc.gov/2020019782

Cover design: Wiley
Cover Photograph: © Cliff Hackel

Printed in the United States of America

V10019798_071520

For Zena and Caparino Z

Contents

Contents

Acknowledgments

My guiding light and inspiration for this book is Sara Sutton, a leader in the field of remote work. My deep and heartfelt thanks to Sara for always being available to answer my questions and to lend her expertise.

Sara is the CEO and founder of FlexJobs, a groundbreaking career website focusing on telecommuting, flexible, freelance, and part-time job listings, and founder of Remote.co, a resource for remote teams and companies. She graciously opened up the vault to allow me to access her list of great companies for remote workers.

A huge cheer to the following workplace experts who shared their insights with me: Dan Schawbel (danschawbel.com), author of *Back to Human* and a Millennial and Gen X career and workplace expert; Sharon Emek, founder of Work at Home Vintage Experts (WAHVE.com), a site for professionals over 50 who work from home for over 300 insurance and accounting firms; and Steve Dalton, program director for daytime career services at Duke University's Fuqua School of Business and author of *The 2-Hour Job Search: Using Technology to Get the Right Job Faster.*

Special nod to Beverly Jones, an executive career coach and author of *Think Like an Entrepreneur, Act Like a CEO*, my go-to expert on all things career-related and a good friend.

My deep gratitude to my agent, Linda Konner, of the Linda Konner Literary Agency, whose publishing vision and faith in my work has driven my mission of empowering people to practically improve their working lives.

My sincere appreciation to former John Wiley & Sons editor Michael Henton for embracing *Great Pajama Jobs* and making the smooth handoff to the thoughtful and engaging editor Kevin Harreld. Gratitude to Jean-Karl Martin, associate marketing manager at Wiley, for his insights on how to employ marketing resources to bring readers the information they need at this unprecedented time. A warm thanks to Purvi Patel, my project editor, and Susan Cerra, Wiley managing editor, who led the production of this book with smooth and clear direction. And a rousing shout-out to my superb copy editor, Amy Handy, for polishing and perfecting every page with care. Beula Jaculin, production editor, carried us to the finish line with aplomb.

The Wiley design team once again fashioned an outstanding book jacket that projects the advice within, with a boost from the spur-of-the-moment photo image by photographer Cliff Hackel, shot in a simple country cottage in Boston, Virginia, one cold Sunday morning (with fashion styling by Caitlin Bonney).

Special credit to Richard Eisenberg, the managing editor of NextAvenue.org. Rich has been making my work smarter and sharper for years and a trove of the work I've done on the subject of remote work was developed with Rich for Next Avenue. Plus, we are both remote workers, so we have that going for us.

On a personal note, my writing and work depends on the support of my family and friends. These include my mom, Marguerite Hannon; the Bonney family: Paul, Pat, Christine, Mike, Caitlin, Shannon, Garrett Goon, Eileen Roach, and Lindsay Corner; the Hannon family: Mike, Judy, Brendan, Sean, Conor, and Brian and Charmaine; the Hersch family: Ginny, David, Corey, and Amy; and the Hackel family: Stu, Sue, Cassie, and Eric. And my best gal pal, Marcy Holquist.

Big thank you to my horse set at Woodhall Farm, especially trainer Peter Foley and Amy Zettler, and, of course, my special horse with the heart of gold, Caparino Z, for bringing balance to my life.

Zena, my super-pooch, gets the shiniest star for always getting me up and going at dawn and accompanying me wherever my laptop goes.

Finally, much love to my remarkable husband, Cliff, who knows what it's like to work from home and helps us find joy in every day.

About the Author

Photo credit: Elizabeth Dranitzke

Kerry Hannon is a leading authority and strategist on career transitions, entrepreneurship, personal finance, and retirement. She is a frequent TV and radio commentator and is a sought-after keynote speaker at conferences.

Kerry is the best-selling and award-winning author of 14 books, including *Never Too Old to Get Rich: The Entrepreneur's Guide to Starting a Business Mid-Life*, published by John Wiley & Sons in 2019, a number one bestseller on Amazon and selected by the *Washington Post* for its Book-of-the-Month Club.

Other best-selling and award-winning books penned by Kerry include *Money Confidence: Really Smart Financial Moves for Newly Single Women, Great Jobs for Everyone 50+: Finding Work That Keeps You*

Happy and Healthy . . . and Pays the Bills, Love Your Job: The New Rules for Career Happiness, Getting the Job You Want after 50, and *What's Next?: Finding Your Passion and Your Dream Job in Your Forties, Fifties, and Beyond.*

Kerry is currently an expert columnist and regular contributor to *The New York Times, MarketWatch,* and *Forbes,* and is the PBS website NextAvenue.org personal finance and entrepreneur expert. Her areas of expertise include entrepreneurship, personal finance, retirement, wealth management, and career transition. Her advice as a work and jobs expert is a regular feature in AARP publications.

Kerry lives in Washington, D.C., with her husband, documentary producer and editor Cliff Hackel, and her Labrador retriever, Zena. Follow Kerry on Twitter @KerryHannon, visit her website at KerryHannon.com, and check out her LinkedIn profile at www .linkedin.com/in/kerryhannon.

Also by Kerry Hannon

Never Too Old to Get Rich: The Entrepreneur's Guide to Starting a Business at Mid-Life

Great Jobs for Everyone 50+, Updated edition: *Finding Work That Keeps You Happy and Healthy . . . and Pays the Bills*

Money Confidence: Really Smart Financial Moves for Newly Single Women

Getting the Job You Want After 50 for Dummies

Love Your Job: The New Rules for Career Happiness

Great Jobs for Everyone 50+: Finding Work That Keeps You Happy and Healthy . . . and Pays the Bills

What's Next: Follow Your Passion and Find Your Dream Job

Suddenly Single: Money Skills for Divorcees and Widows

Introduction

love my job. I log in to my computer in the quiet predawn from my comfy couch with a steaming mug of black coffee and get to work tout de suite.

This spring, in what felt like a blink of an eye, remote work suddenly was thrust onto many workers and employers who had never wished for this to be the only work option. And there were millions of workers like me, logging into the office without the commute, not because they wanted to, but because they had no choice.

The coronavirus has radically changed our workplaces. Unprecedented, unprepared, and uncharted, working from home became the norm. Adjust and get on with it. Kids scrambling underfoot, teenagers sitting at the table beside us engaged in their online classrooms, ramping up tech skills to make virtual connections, feeling isolated. Oh boy, all of the above became a stark and somewhat frightening reality for many workers.

Everyone in the world has been impacted by this pandemic. And our workplaces may be changed forever. As I finish this manuscript, there is no way to predict our future. But this I do foresee: An increasing number of employers will become remote-friendly and probably institute a formal remote work policy. During the mandated time with offices shuttered, they'll have recognized the benefits of having remote workers.

"An ongoing, formal shift in the way people can work will happen in stages as it becomes increasingly clear a return to 'normal' won't happen overnight," says Cali Williams Yost, chief strategist and futurist at Flex+Strategy Group. "After a year to a year and a half of remote and flexible working, it will be part of the 'way we work here' cultural DNA, and there will be no going back," she says. "Then the flexible work genie will be officially out of the bottle, and all employees will benefit beyond the crisis."

Not surprisingly, in a Gallup national poll conducted in April, three in five U.S. workers who had been doing their jobs from home during the coronavirus pandemic said they would prefer to continue to work remotely as much as possible, once public health restrictions are lifted.

And a study from economics professors Jonathan Dingel and Brent Neiman of the University of Chicago estimates that while less than a quarter of all full-time employees worked from home at least sometimes before the pandemic, *37 percent of jobs could be done entirely from home.*

That said, industries where telework is a practical option at the moment tend to employ better-educated workers—fields like professional, scientific, and technical services, as well as finance and management, according to the report. Among the ones least flexible for telework: retail trade and food service, which typically employ sizable numbers of low-wage older workers.

"I don't think there will ever be a company again that doesn't consider that some element of emergency preparedness has to be made and working remotely in some form needs to be addressed and hopefully turned into a formalized policy," Sara Sutton, founder and CEO of the job boards FlexJobs and Remote.co, tells me.

"It is the tipping point for work from home as a valid and important component of a healthy organization and not just good for the worker. Having a remote component is never going to be doubted again, or looked at as fringe."

Meanwhile, the enforced work-from-home scenario, for those of you who have never considered it, may have triggered a desire to keep it going after the pandemic resolves itself.

I have never before talked to so many workers who adapted to using communication technology like Zoom conferencing and are embracing it, no longer intimidated or frustrated by screen-to-screen meetings and virtual meet-ups to chat with co-workers. They feel empowered.

My goal in writing this book is to help workers find a great remote job. Many of you may now have one—whether you opted in or not. If that's the case, skip to my workshop in Part III for advice on how to succeed as a remote worker over the long haul.

Each of us has unique work requirements and personalities, so use my advice as motivation. You will ultimately develop your own remote work recipe that suits you and, importantly, your manager and your employer's needs.

I work for several employers, but it's all virtual, and I have for a long, long time. How it works for me will differ from what works for you, but there is a spine of wisdom that you will find here that you can mold to make your own secret sauce.

The Changing Face of Remote Work

Even before the COVID-19, working from home was steadily gaining a head of steam for workers of all ages. Over the last five years, U.S. workers working remotely grew 44 percent to around 4.7 million, according to research by job board Flexjobs.com in partnership with Global Workplace Analytics.

Gallup research conducted before the onset of COVID-19 showed that 43 percent of employees worked remotely in some capacity. In a study conducted by Condeco Software, 41 percent of global businesses surveyed said they already offered some degree of remote working. Upwork's "Future Workforce Report" predicted that 73 percent of all teams will have remote workers by 2028, a percentage that may even be on the conservative side in the aftermath of the 2020 stay-at-home mandates.

Fueling the trend pre-COVID-19: In a survey from global outplacement and executive and business coaching firm Challenger, Gray & Christmas, Inc., 70 percent of employers reported they were having trouble finding applicants with the necessary qualifications. To attract talent, 62 percent were offering remote work options.

"Employers are having trouble finding workers with the skills needed to perform their duties," says Andrew Challenger, vice president of Challenger, Gray & Christmas, Inc. "If this continues, it could hurt the bottom line and limit expansion. As employees, especially Millennials and Gen Z workers, demand more work/life balance, employers will find they must respond with these offerings."

Who doesn't yearn for flexible work schedules, a shuffle to the next room as a commute, and the fundamental joy of working away in the most basic of business-casual clothing—our pajamas.

In all seriousness, though, autonomy is one of the key components of loving a job, as I found when I wrote my book, *Love Your Job: The New Rules of Career Happiness.* Working remotely is an important way you can capture the elusive psychological feeling of freedom and personal independence. And there's a bottom-line benefit as well—it saves money that you might spend on commuting costs for transportation, meals and coffee out, work clothes, and the list goes on.

"More and more people are working remotely because they want flexibility over their schedule and where, when, and how they work," Dan Schawbel (danschawbel.com), author of *Back to Human* and a Millennial and Gen X career and workplace expert, told me, again before the workplace shifted this spring. "And corporations benefit from a recruiting and retention standpoint by offering it, plus they save money on real estate costs. Both employees and employers win."

This year, spurred by the coronavirus pandemic, "has been the 'grand remote work experiment' where people who have never worked remotely are for the first time and are benefitting from it," Schawbel told me. "During this time, companies were being forced to allow their employees to work remotely for health and safety reasons, so they are developing the policies they should have had years ago."

Technology has enabled people to work from Bali to Boston, regardless of where their boss is situated, and this year's cataclysmic necessity has borne that out. Importantly, they can hold on to a job when a partner or spouse is transferred to another posting, which is particularly germane to military spouses. (More on employers offering remote positions aimed at military spouses in Chapter 8.)

Video conferencing, texting, and other collaborative tools have blown open the door to the workplace. "In the future, remote work options will be as common as healthcare coverage," Schawbel says. "It will be sought after and almost a benefit requirement. Employers that don't offer flexibility will not be able to compete for the top talent. Many younger workers and friends I know are willing to work for less money if they can work remotely. They're asking about it in their interviews."

Back in 2007, when Schawbel created one of the first social media positions at a Fortune 200 company, he asked his manager if he could work from home at least occasionally. "I justified not being in the office because I could conduct all of my social media responsibilities remotely," Schawbel recalls. "I had created and managed the company's Facebook, LinkedIn, and Twitter accounts while contributing to their internal social media platform and helping various departments run campaigns. My manager wouldn't give me permission to work from home because, as he said, 'it would make your teammates jealous.' If my manager had responded by granting me the privilege to work from home, my employment situation might have sufficed and I would have stayed with the company longer."

For those of you at mid-life, after years of commuting to an office, a work-from-home position can, in fact, be a dream job, and you may have just discovered that joy. It is for me. The top four reported reasons people seek remote work, according to an analysis by FlexJobs.com, are work-life balance (75 percent), family (45 percent), time savings (42 percent), and commute stress (41 percent). Other high-ranking factors for seeking flexible work options include avoiding office politics and distractions (33 percent), travel (29 percent), cost savings (25 percent), being a pet owner (24 percent), having caregiving responsibilities (18 percent), and living in a bad local job market (15 percent).

"Older workers want to retire from the office, not the job," says Sharon Emek, founder of Work at Home Vintage Experts (WAHVE.com), a site for professionals over 50 who work from home for over 300 insurance and accounting firms. "Meantime, employers are looking for people they do not need to train."

Getting Started

One of the easiest ways to stay in the workforce as you age, or as life events shift for you (a marriage, a spouse transfer, caring for children or aging relatives, a health issue) is to have a great pajama job, as I like to refer to working remotely. This has been my mode of work for many years now, albeit not always clad in pjs. And I admit, I'm far from retired at 59, but I find the autonomy of working outside of an office environment suits my lifestyle.

Landing a job that's a great fit for both parties is rarely an easy endeavor, and that's especially true for one where an employee is working out of a manager's sight on a regular basis. There's a bond of trust and commitment that is integral to make these work relationships thrive.

You aren't reinventing yourself in order to work from home, you are redeploying. You already have many of the skills in your wheelhouse right now that will help make it work for you. These include organizational skills, an ability to focus, self-discipline, communication skills (both verbal and written), time-management skills, and a self-reliant ability to work independently.

Tech skills are especially important when you work remotely, and that might mean learning new computer programs and communication tools, such as web conferencing, video chats, and other tools, and making sure typing skills are up to par. The ability to troubleshoot minor computer and technical issues can also come in handy.

And it goes without saying that you have to be comfortable working without a pal to pop around the corner to kibitz with to break up the day. Importantly, you have to really want to continue to work—not to just dabble in it.

The hundreds of remote workers I have interviewed have told me what I already know firsthand, that it takes discipline, but the time flexibility to do things such as nonwork hobbies, volunteering, or simply the joy of working with their dog nestled under their desk (as I often do with my Labrador retriever, Zena) is what makes it worthwhile.

Another, lesser-known aspect to chuck into the pro column: When you work remotely, your "age" is not necessarily the deal breaker it can be when you're front and center in the workplace, face to face. Truth. And that holds true for those in their 20s as well as those in their 60s and over.

In this book you will find my strategic advice on how to land a remote job, to love it and make it work for you. This includes:

- *Do the inner soul-searching.* Not everyone is hard-wired to be a remote worker. "You need to be honest with yourself," Sutton tells me. "Are you self-disciplined, focused, organized, skilled at time-management? You must be able to set boundaries around your work environment with friends, family, neighbors, or when working in a co-working space and not being distracted all the time."

  Are you tech-savvy, open to learning new tools, and comfortable fixing minor technical problems? They will arise.

  Do you thrive off of the stimulation of office colleagues buzzing around you? One of the biggest hurdles for remote workers is loneliness. "If it's going to be a real con for you, and you can feel it in your gut that it will be hard for you not to have that interaction and action environment, then don't consider remote work," Sutton advises. "Part-time or a flexible schedule might be better."

I agree with Sutton. Succeeding as a remote worker really is an individual effort. If you're in your 20s and 30s, an office environment can be fantastic. You build friendships and a lifelong network. I loved working with colleagues during my 20s and 30s in the *Forbes* magazine office in Greenwich Village and at the *U.S. News & World Report* headquarters on the edge of Georgetown in Washington, D.C.

Many of those relationships remain strong today. I could not have achieved what I have in my career if I had not had that in-office experience and learning opportunity from the veterans who mentored me and those with whom I shared bylines and reporting duties along the way. Those long days and eyeball-to-eyeball interactions formed the spine of my work ethic and solidly built my career trajectory.

But for someone who has young children, or is an introvert, remote duties might be the perfect ticket to achieving a balanced approach to productive work. And for those gliding, or phasing, into retirement, or working part-time in retirement, the freedom to work remotely is a benefit you can't put a price tag on.

That said, you can put a cost savings on some of the basics. The researchers at FlexJobs estimate that the average person could save around $4,000 a year by working from home. Dry cleaning and laundering ($500–$1,500) ranked as one of the largest costs of working from an office, as well as lunches and coffee ($1,040). Commuting also factored in, with items like gas ($686) or car maintenance ($767) costing additional money over the year.

- *Connect, connect, connect.* The very best remote workers will reach out to co-workers and managers regularly. "A key skill companies who hire remote workers are looking for is communication," Sutton says. "You need to be able to say, hey, I'm a little confused about this, or hey, can you help clarify this for me? You have to take responsibility and speak up. If you're not visible, it's hard for your manager to know something's wrong."

Network with people you know at remote-friendly employers where you'd like to work. UnitedHealth Group, Kelly Services,

Amazon, Robert Half International, GitLab, and Dell are among the leading companies regularly hiring for remote jobs. Xerox, American Express, and about two dozen other Fortune 500 companies have made entire divisions remote. (See Part II for a deeper dive.)

You might go straight to a company you'd like to work for, maybe even your current employer, and see if it hires remote workers. A good place to start is the career section of the company's website.

- *Take the time to research.* Online job boards like Flexjobs.com, Remote.co, and WAHVE.com connect employers with workers who are focused on legitimate work-from-home jobs and prescreen each job and employer to be certain they aren't scams. Other popular remote job boards to check out are Rat Race Rebellion, Working Nomads, We Work Remotely, Skip The Drive, Jobspresso, Sidehusl and ZipRecruiter, and even UpWork regular gigs (more on these in Chapter 5).

FlexJobs, for one, reports that its remote job listings grew 52 percent in the past two years; the most common and top career fields offering remote work are sales, medical and health, education and training, customer service, and computer and information technology.

Job titles range from customer service representative to program manager to teacher, accounting (bookkeepers, CFOs, controllers, etc.), administrative assistants, virtual assistants, medical transcriptionists, remote nurses, pharmacists, radiologists, and data entry. Pay ranges from $18/hour to $40/hour or more, depending on the level of the job and the experience. (See Part I.)

"Search on the job boards for skills you have and passions outside of titles," Sutton says. "Be a little experimental with it. If you're in data analytics, but also love biking, type in those words and see what comes up. With remote work, it is really helpful if you're passionate about what you're doing, and it's not just punching a clock That will keep you motivated when you are working solo."

- *Focus on a few employers.* "These remote jobs are increasingly competitive," Sutton says. "I encourage job seekers to put out fewer applications, but for jobs they really feel strongly about. Instead of doing 100 applications, do 10 for the ones you

really, really want. Thoroughly investigate the company. Write
in the cover letter that you admire x, y, z things they are doing.
You can find these newsy items on their website press page or
company culture page. This is your first impression, and you
want to show you care. And if you know someone who works at
the firm, toss out their name there, too."
- *Watch out for scams.* There are a variety and abundance of jobs
that are all career categories from entry level to executive. "But
for every legitimate work-from-home job, there are dozens of
job scams. Google the company name and the word "scam" and
see what comes up, Sutton advises. "That's not proof, but you
will see if there is chatter about the quality of the company."

Some States Actively Promote Remote Work

Fed up with living in an expensive city or community? Eager to bring
your stress level down? Interested in working hours you prefer and
from your home? That may sound like a TV infomercial, but the fact
is that working remotely in a low-cost area is becoming easier at a
time when it's also becoming more appealing.

New programs in Savannah, Georgia, Tulsa, Oklahoma, and
Vermont have been rolling out to lure new residents who'd work
from there remotely. Also, new and growing websites are helping
people find jobs where they can work from home, wherever that
may be, as I mentioned above.

"Advances in technology such as high-speed internet and Wi-Fi
over the last ten to fifteen years definitely make it easier to work outside of the office," says Sutton. "And more people are knowledge
workers, meaning that they work with ideas and information, rather
than with machinery. The knowledge economy naturally supports
jobs that can be done from home."

Offering workplace flexibility through remote work is one way
that employers can retain and attract skilled workers, and also "keep
the trains running" as we all navigate the rapid shift toward telecommuting during the pandemic and its aftermath. Plus, there's the
bottom-line payback: By letting more workers work from home, businesses and nonprofits can reduce the cost of office space and equipment and see productivity improvements.

The payback is often more than money. "A study we conducted
in the IT division of a Fortune 500 company shows that a shift to

more flexible work practices—those that give employees more control over when and where they work and convey support for employees' personal lives—benefits workers without hurting business performance," says Phyllis Moen, whom I interviewed for an article in the *AARP Bulletin*. Moen is a professor of sociology at the University of Minnesota and co-author of *Overload: How Good Jobs Went Bad and What We Can Do About It.* "Instead," she explains, "employees we studied describe feeling less stressed, more energized, and more satisfied with their jobs. The company benefits, too, because employees are less likely to experience burnout and less likely to look for other jobs, quit, or retire early."

"Companies who want to keep talent are accommodating them," says Emek, of WAHVE (Work at Home Vintage Experts). "And often they can't find talent within driving distance to their office."

The explosion of remote jobs means that many workers have more options in choosing where they live, how they commute, and which profession to follow. "The most notable change we've seen over the past year is not so much the growth in the sheer volume of remote job listings, but the growth in the variety of remote job titles these companies are seeking to hire," says Sutton. "Companies are expanding the range of professional positions they're allowing to work from home."

Some cities and states are also finding that the lure of remote work (plus new initiatives offering cash grants) entices people of all ages to move there. FlexJobs is partnering with economic development groups in Kentucky, Colorado, Utah, New Mexico, Kansas, and Florida to help residents get remote jobs.

Tulsa, rolled out its Tulsa Remote initiative to lure new residents by offering them $10,000 grants for a year to work from there remotely, plus other benefits.

The enterprise provides co-working space for the year at 36 Degrees North, Tulsa's basecamp for entrepreneurs, and offers monthly meetups and workshops to develop skills and strategies for working remotely effectively. Program participants also have the option of living in a new, fully furnished apartment for a discounted rent, plus free utilities for the first three months.

Backed by the Tulsa-based nonprofit George Kaiser Family Foundation, the goal is to bring in people who'll stick around, get involved in the community, strengthen the local economy, and maybe ultimately launch businesses locally.

Tulsa Remote received nearly 1,000 applications the first day it opened in 2019 and capped the total at 10,000, a number the program received within 10 weeks. In 2020, the program was scheduled to triple in size to welcome between 250 and 300 new Tulsans.

Vermont launched a Remote Worker Grant Program, paying about 100 people $10,000 each over two years to cover expenses for moving to the state and working remotely. Qualifying expenses include the cost of relocation, computer software or hardware, broadband access or upgrade, and membership in a co-working or similar space.

A bill introduced by neighboring Massachusetts Governor Charles D. Baker includes a tax credit of up to $2,000 per employee for companies that support employees who work from home or remote locations ($50 million annually has been allocated for the credit).

These initiatives started for several reasons, including bolstering the local economies, bringing jobs to rural or economically disadvantaged areas, or in the case of new initiatives in Massachusetts, for example, addressing the infrastructure and productivity problems caused by excessive commuter traffic.

Sometimes, new remote-work opportunities come out of frustration, like April Goettle's new website for Nebraskans, remoter.tech. "Personal pain is a great motivator to find good solutions," she says.

Goettle had been weary of driving three hours a day, five days a week from her home in Lyons, Nebraska, to her job as a website graphic designer in Omaha, 75 miles away. "I needed a tech job, and that is just the way it was," she says. She wanted to work for a local company and be part of the Omaha tech boom.

When she began looking for Nebraska companies who'd hire rural workers looking for remote-work tech jobs, Goettle was shocked that none of the Omaha job boards offered such links.

So she created Remoter.tech, and began a campaign to convince smaller start-up tech firms in Omaha and surrounding rural areas to post open remote positions there. Remoter.tech aims to be a bulletin board for web designers, graphic designers, engineers, project managers, data analytic experts, and content creators.

"My focus is on providing resources for people who are trying to have a lower cost of living and work/life balance in a small community and have good-paying jobs in the Omaha area," Goettle says.

"In the Midwest, and where I am from in Montana, communities are struggling to keep the population. On the other end of the spectrum, we have towns like Omaha struggling with their hiring needs. But it's not a common practice to hire remote. It seemed to me like two problems that had a related solution."

How to Use This Book

Working from home is *here*, and it's real. In *Great Pajama Jobs*, I show you:

- How to find a great remote job and a great employer
- How to create a great remote worker résumé
- Great ways to showcase your skills
- How to get past the electronic screeners when applying for a position online
- Best practices to avoid scams

Great Pajama Jobs is your playbook to inspire you to find the freedom of working remotely and earn a paycheck doing work you love and are skilled at doing. The range of opportunities is astonishingly varied, ranging from coder to transcriptionist to virtual assistant to customer service to translator.

In this book, you will find:

- Up-to-date resources for finding a solid work-from-home job
- Practical work-from-home jobs, with the nitty-gritty details, pay range, and qualifications required
- My workshop, teeming with information to help you land that perfect work-from-home job, including a résumé revamp, best online job boards for home-based positions, how to beat the automated screening systems, organizing a productive home office, time-management tips, networking advice, tax counsel, and help with saving for retirement
- A go-to list of great work-from-home companies
- Advice on how to avoid work-from-home scams
- A newfound perspective on working from home and what it offers beyond avoiding the typical 9–5 daily commute
- Tips for collaboration, scheduling meetings, and sharing ideas even when someone can't meet face to face

In these pages, you will discover the ultimate guide to great remote jobs, where to find them, pay ranges, and qualifications needed. I'll give you the action steps to take to find a job that works for you and guidance on how to succeed as a remote worker.

Great Pajama Jobs is divided into three parts:

- Part I profiles work-from-home jobs. You'll find lots of professional occupations and some that may require retraining and adding a degree or certificate. And you'll also find a large selection of jobs geared for someone who wants a little income but doesn't want to do much heavy lifting. Many of these jobs offer flexible schedules—a week, a month, a few months a year, or even on-again, off-again contract work, as well as full-time positions. Don't be put off by the random jump from a professional full-time position to a more casual part-time retirement one.

  Each entry in this section follows this format: the nitty-gritty, the pay range, and the qualifications needed, with a smattering of job-hunting tips tossed in. Note that pay ranges vary widely from employer to employer and city to city and by your experience; they are listed here as a guideline.

- Part II presents snapshots of companies with a history of offering solid work-from-home positions. These firms are industry leaders in supporting remote employees to create partnerships where both employee and employer succeed.

- Part III is "Kerry's Great Pajama Jobs Workshop," with advice on finding a great work-from-home job using specific tools: résumés, interviews, social media, and networking savvy. It includes a section on the nuts and bolts of how to work from home productively and profitably, paying taxes, saving for retirement, the inner quest to find work/life balance, dealing with loneliness and isolation, managing your time effectively, and more.

I deliver the professional advice and strategies I've been doling out as a career strategist and as a retirement and personal finance expert and journalist for more than three decades with thousands of followers and millions of readers.

I have developed this material through extensive reporting and interviews conducted for my expert columns that appear on Next Avenue, *Forbes, MarketWatch, The New York Times,* and AARP.

Those outlets have allowed me to get a conversation going with thousands of people to see what kind of advice they want and what really helps.

My advice also stems from the worries that I hear from audience members at the end of one of my keynote speeches, or during a panel discussion at a conference, or when a listener calls into a radio talk show where I am a guest to ask a question, or when someone calls or emails for one-on-one career guidance.

These requests for advice persuaded me that there's a burning need for this kind of frank career direction.

You can dip in and out of the chapters as they apply to your situation. Throughout, you'll find websites, job boards, and books to help your search.

There's something here for everyone, a remote job-hunter's smorgasbord. My aim is to help you discover job possibilities that spur your imagination about how you can make the most of your talents to create work that, well, works for you.

At the very heart of it, I wrote this book to help you find the work you love with the flexibility that will help you prosper.

Kick off your slippers, let's go job hunting!

P A R T

GREAT PAJAMA JOBS

You may want a full-time job that can lead to promotions and career advancement, or a job for a season, for a stint of living in a different country or city for a few years, or one that will allow you to gradually unwind into retirement, or even a job that you clock into for a few hours a week to stay engaged and relevant. You may even strategically build an income stream from a tapestry of work-from-home jobs you enjoy and are skilled at doing.

Many remote workers I have interviewed say they aren't looking for high-pay, stressful management positions on the frontlines. Others say that's not so, but don't see why being in an office setting can help them perform better.

Deciding What (Else) You Want Out of Work

Flexible work enables employees to effectively manage their work-life responsibilities, leading to better outcomes in both spheres.

Talk with enough happy workers and you'll find the secret is a job that offers flexibility. For my book *Love Your Job: The New Rules for Career Happiness*, I interviewed hundreds of workers about what made them love their jobs. Flexibility and a sense of freedom and autonomy ranks high.

And happy translates into productivity on the job: 83 percent of global companies report an improvement in employee productivity after adopting flexible work policies and 61 percent report a rise in profits, according to a study involving 8,000 global employees and employers. The majority of employers with flexible workplace policies also say it has had a positive impact on their organization's reputation and helps retain valuable workers and recruit the best candidates.

For Sandra Molleck, 54, who works as a commercial lines account manager for a large California-based insurance company, the biggest rewards of working from home are "no commute, no drama, no purchasing expensive work clothes (and especially nylons), plus a comfortable and quiet work environment," she tells me. Her biggest challenges: "Getting into a routine and staying away from snacks," says Molleck. "It took me a while, but I have a set schedule. I work out before work and on my lunch hour."

What motivates us to work and what each of us calls a "great pajama job" is as individual as we are. "Different flavors of ice cream," as my sister, Pat, likes to say. But I implore you: Try to find a job you love and that challenges you. It will make all the difference in your health as well as your wealth.

While Gen Zers believe they are hardworking, one in four (26 percent) admit they would work harder and stay longer at a company that supports flexible schedules, with flexibility desired most in Canada (33 percent), the U.K. (31 percent), and the United States (31 percent). That's according to a global survey conducted by the Workforce Institute at Kronos Incorporated of 3,400 members of Generation Z across 12 countries.

It's easier to create flexible programs as a startup or small business, which gives them the advantage over large global enterprises that have to take many factors into consideration and change long-standing corporate cultures rooted in the status quo, says Dan Schawbel author of *Back to Human*.

Overall, people want control over how, when, and where they work and will seek an employment situation that satisfies that need, even if it means sacrificing pay, healthcare benefits, a team, free coffee, and office space.

In general, remote jobs come in two broad categories. The first are conventional professional jobs that are full-time or part-time, which pay you a salary or set hourly rate on a regular basis. You're part of a team. And you may be entitled to traditional employee benefits: health insurance, paid vacation time, an employer-sponsored retirement plan. The only difference is where you do your work.

The second type of remote work comes under the umbrella of freelance, consultant, or contractor positions. Typically, you have more control over when and where you work and how much, but you are in charge of paying your quarterly taxes and shelling out for health insurance. And when you go on vacation, you don't get paid. Pay can be project-based or hourly.

In the following pages, you'll find a plethora of professional occupations, some that may demand retraining and adding a degree or certificate. And you'll also find a selection of jobs geared for someone who wants a little income but doesn't want a full-blown commitment on a daily basis.

There are adaptable schedules, from a few days a week to a few months a year to a steady gig, or even one you might consider launching as a home-based business. Each job description follows this format: the nitty-gritty, pay range, and qualifications needed, with a smattering of job-hunting tips tossed in.

I've structured the snapshots roughly by career field: creative, financial, education, tech, and healthcare. Of course, pay will depend on myriad factors from the employer to your own negotiating moxie, but I've provided averages to give you a sense of current demand.

While remote work exists in most career fields, it is growing more quickly in some fields than in others. With that in mind, FlexJobs analyzed more than 50 career categories in its database to figure out which remote career categories have grown at a high rate.

Seven of the fastest-growing remote job fields are art and creative, bookkeeping, internet and ecommerce, K–12 education, graphic design, translation, math, and economics. Leading job titles include accountant, engineer (civil, mechanical, electrical, etc.), teacher or faculty, writer, consultant, program manager, project manager, customer service representative, business development manager, account manager, and executive.

In the following chapter you will find snapshots of remote jobs that allow you to work from home either entirely or part of the time.

Remote jobs are also known as telecommuting jobs, virtual jobs, and work-from-home jobs. This list is culled from ones from my extensive research on legitimate remote positions.

My aim is to help you explore remote jobs that suit your goals, ambitions, and life stage. It is by no means a definitive list, but a starter kit for you to begin your personal exploration. As employers accept the power and possibilities that remote teams can add to their success, great new pajama jobs are popping up all the time. Let's roll.

Great Remote Jobs

Art Director

The nitty-gritty: Style and creative magic with a dose of management savvy as you ensure that the trains run on time for project deadlines and reaching goals is your mojo. The end product may appear in print magazines or online websites, packaging for products, web advertising and online promotions for products and services, video games, and more. You craft the overall visual path with input from your team of designers. A growing area of opportunity is web design for a company's website.

Pay range: An art director salary typically falls between $98,937 and $132,784, according to Salary.com. Average hourly wages are between $48 and $64.

Qualifications: A bachelor's degree in art or a related area and earlier work experience as a graphic designer is generally a prerequisite. And increasingly, most positions today require that experience to be within the realm of digital or online media publishing. Employers run the gamut from advertising agencies to publishers to movie production companies. Some art directors earn a master of fine arts (MFA) degree to supplement their work experience. And you can't just be lost in your artistic vision; the ability to listen and translate your concepts to your employer and other artists and staff working alongside is essential.

Voice-over Artist

The nitty-gritty: The need for voice talent is rising due to the ramp up in multimedia websites and audiobooks, podcasts, and so forth. The diversity of jobs an employer might need you to master range from commercials to web videos, audiobooks, documentaries, business and training videos, telephone messages, and applications. Keep in mind this is typically a part-time position.

Pay range: The average salary for a voice-over artist is $50 per hour, according to the job board Indeed.com.

Qualifications: If you're working from your home office, you'll probably have to shell out for the proper equipment such as recording software, a microphone, and headsets. You'll also need a professional demo to share with potential clients. Training as an actor or public speaking skills are a plus. Some websites to tap are Voice123.com and Voices.com. To get higher-paying voice-over jobs, you may need to join a union such as SAG-AFTRA, the combination of the Screen Actors Guild and the American Federation of Television and Radio Artists. Union fees will depend on your market.

Interior Designer

The nitty-gritty: Interior designers style indoor spaces that are functional, safe, and beautiful for almost every type of structure. Your canvas is space that you imbue with colors, appropriate lighting and furniture, floor and wall coverings, and finishes, even plumbing fixtures. A working knowledge of reading blueprints is expected. You generally should be up to speed on building codes and regulations. And importantly, you must manage your client's expectations and estimate costs for the project as well as problem-solve to navigate challenges stemming from construction delays or unobtainability of certain materials. You'll be in charge of ordering the materials and supervising the installation of the design components. This is not a solo show. In many cases, you're part of a team that includes architects, engineers, skilled craftspeople, and construction workers. One caveat: If you go the residential route, you might want to do some soul-searching to be sure you enjoy spending a lot of time in strangers' houses.

Pay range: The average salary for an interior designer is $48,810, according to Payscale.com. Hourly pay ranges are above $35.26 an hour.

Qualifications: Coursework should include classes in interior design, drawing, and computer-aided design (CAD). Linda LaMagna, whom I wrote about in my book, *Never Too Old to Get Rich: The Entrepreneur's Guide to Starting a Business Mid-Life,* made a career transition in her 50s from medical sales to interior design. To do so, she enrolled in an online program that consisted of 12 courses – everything from colors and textiles to using software to build rooms. In three months, she was awarded a diploma in interior design from the Interior Design Institute (theinteriordesigninstitute.com). Programs in interior design are available at the associate's, bachelor's, and master's degree levels. The National Association of Schools of Art and Design accredits more than 360 postsecondary colleges, universities, and independent institutes that have programs in art and design. The Council for Interior Design Accreditation (accredit-id.org) accredits about 180 professional-level (bachelor's or master's degree) interior design programs. The National Kitchen & Bath Association recognizes kitchen and bath design specialty programs (certificate, associate's degree, and bachelor's degree levels) in nearly 100 colleges and universities. Licensure requirements vary by state. Most interior designers use computer-aided design (CAD) software for their drawings. Throughout the design process, interior designers often use building information modeling (BIM) software to create three-dimensional visualizations that include construction elements such as walls or roofs, according to the Bureau of Labor Statistics' Occupational Outlook Handbook.

You might specialize in specific types of buildings, residential, medical, or hotels, even precise rooms, such as bathrooms or kitchens. Corporate designers create interior designs for professional workplaces. Healthcare designers plan and renovate healthcare centers, clinics, doctors' offices, hospitals, and residential care facilities. Kitchen and bath designers focus on kitchens and bathrooms and have expert understanding of cabinet, fixture, appliance, plumbing, and electrical needs. Sustainable designers are keen on devising ways to improve energy and water efficiencies and indoor air quality, as well as using environmentally sustainable products.

Certification in Leadership in Energy and Environmental Design (LEED) from the U.S. Green Building Council indicates expertise in designing buildings and spaces with sustainable practices in mind. Finally, universal designers revamp spaces to make them more accessible for an aging population or those with disabilities. Possible employers include home furnishings stores, architectural firms, and commercial and residential real estate development firms.

Move Manager

The nitty-gritty: You're the master of coordinating a move and planning a new home setup. Your clients may need advice on selecting the furniture, artwork, china, collectibles, and household goods that will fit well in the new home. And you help make decisions on what can be sold, donated, or given to friends and family. You might even be in charge of making suggestions for new furniture, or managing an estate or yard sale. Possible employers are assisted-care living communities, corporations that regularly move employees to different locations, and real estate firms.

Pay range: Fees can range from $30 per hour to $75+.

Qualifications: Knowledge of interior design is essential. An "in" with a local realtor can spur your business, as well as deliver a steady clientele down the road. An unruffled but take-charge demeanor is a preferred personality quality. This type of move is full of emotion. For more information on courses and certification, contact the National Association of Senior Move Managers (nasmm.org). You must be empathetic, but hard-nosed.

Job hunting tips: Visit local realtors' offices and retirement and assisted- living communities in your area to ask about their future residents' needs. Find out who is handling this type of work for them. The community's management office usually provides soon-to-be residents with suggestions for moving specialists to lend a hand.

Graphic Designer

The nitty-gritty: Projects can range from designing letterhead, business cards, and logos for local businesses to creating marketing brochures, flashy websites, and email marketing. Most design work can be done via your home computer. You must be at ease with manipulating computer graphics and design software, and possibly know- how to program animated graphics.

You may, of course, find yourself sketching the old-fashioned way with pad and pen as an inspired idea takes shape. You must be able to translate your concept into words, too. An underlying ability to perceive what appeals to your clients is essential.

This is a collaborative process. Tweaking and redesigns come with the territory. Be prepared for hours at the computer and last-minute crushes for deadlines. A designer might be employed with a variety of industry firms to develop publicity or advertising materials for the organization, or you might find a job with a media company or an advertising or design agency and work with a smorgasbord of clients and projects. Many graphic designers are independent contractors who work from home on a per-project basis.

Pay range: Annual salary of $32,000 to $62,000 and up, according to PayScale.com.

Qualifications: Your success rests on your aptitude for design and capability to meet deadlines. Degree programs in fine arts or graphic design are offered at many colleges, universities, and private design schools. Most curricula include principles of design, computerized design, commercial graphics production, printing techniques, and website design. Associate degrees and certificates in graphic design also are available from two-year and three-year professional schools. The National Association of Schools of Art and Design (nasad.arts-accredit.org) accredits postsecondary institutions with programs in art and design. Some job postings state upfront that you need experience handling clients and are proficient in Adobe Photoshop, Illustrator, and InDesign. You must also be able to execute graphic design requests and communicate effectively with an assigned production team.

Job hunting tips: A go-to resource for career information is the American Institute of Graphic Arts (aiga.org) and the extensive job board on the One Club (oneclub.org) site. Other job sites to scroll through include Coroflot (coroflot.com) and Krop (krop.com). Sample remote graphic design job titles: Illustrator, Designer, Layout Manager.

Writer/Editor/Content Strategist

The nitty-gritty: You don't have to be a professional scribe to find work in this arena. You do need a clear grasp of sentence and paragraph construction, spelling, grammar, and punctuation. Jobs run the gamut from copyediting and proofreading to résumé writing and technical editing. If you have expertise in a particular field or genre, that's all the better for opening doors.

JournalismJobs.com provides a range of postings for part-time writing and editing jobs. Freelance writers can find postings on Freelancer.com or Upwork.com. If you have a LinkedIn profile, you can flag recruiters on the site to send along periodic contract or freelance openings from employers' job postings that suit your experience. You can also set up your own shop to provide these résumé- and essay-tuning services.

For more general writing gigs, you might reach out to local associations and organizations, community newsletters, and other regional publications. Ask if they need an extra hand on an assignment basis for online and print articles, brochures, and press releases. Freelance writers and editors typically set their own schedules based on deadlines.

Pay range: Pay for writers and editors varies widely, depending on type of writing, location, and experience. Few jobs are billed by the hour, though, and instead freelancers are often paid by the project, word count, or even number of visitors to an online article. For creating a polished résumé for a client, you might charge a base fee of $200. Some publishers pay freelance writers by the word or by the article, and that fluctuates widely depending on your background and experience: Anywhere from 50 cents to $3 a word is not out of the ordinary. If you write for an online publisher, you might be paid solely based on the number of times web visitors view your article or if the content is licensed to other publishers.

Qualifications: No formal training is required. Employers often look for expertise in a variety of fields, from healthcare to taxes to résumé writing. For newsier publications, a grasp of the *Associated Press Stylebook* or the *Chicago Manual of Style* might be necessary. Plus, *The Elements of Style* by Strunk and White never goes out of style. The gist of this work is to create clear, compelling copy that is tailored to and engages the audience. Chances are you will tap Microsoft® Office Suite – Word, PowerPoint, and Excel; web-based email; project management; and content management software tools.

Event Planner

The nitty-gritty: It's not all glam and swag bags when you are the one behind the scenes setting the stage. This is a job for the uber-organized, detail-oriented pro. Logistics blend with creativity and a cool demeanor not to be rattled if the best-laid plans start to unravel. Event planners work on a variety of gatherings from corporate get-togethers to birthday celebrations, weddings, and fundraising charity occasions. Employment of meeting, convention, and event planners is projected to grow 7 percent from 2018 to 2028, faster than the average for all occupations.

Pay range: The average hourly pay ranges from $17.57, to higher than $34.43, according to PayScale. Annual salary ranges from $32,000 to $72,000.

Qualifications: Some universities and .community colleges offer degree and certificate programs in event management. You might also consider the Conference and Event Professional Certificate credential, or a Digital Event Strategist certification, both offered by the Professional Convention Management Association, now called PCMA, PCMA.org. Job opportunities should be best for candidates with hospitality experience and a bachelor's degree in meeting and event management, hospitality, or tourism management, according to the Bureau of Labor Statistics. If weddings are your bailiwick, check out the websites of the American Association of Certified Wedding Planners (aacwp.org), the Association of Certified Professional Wedding Consultants (acpwc.com), and The Knot (theknot.com/marketplace/wedding-planners).

Travel Agent

The nitty-gritty: A rising number of travelers want to turn the task of booking travel over to a pro. Traveling planning is a frustrating time suck for most of us, so the do-it-yourself crowd is increasingly looking for a capable helping hand to find great airfares and rentals and to streamline the process. You'll spend a fair amount of time on the phone and doing online research, so this job demands persistence and a creative mind to find solutions. It helps to be a road warrior yourself. Some top employers are American Express Co., AAA Motor Club, and Omega World Travel.

One possible perk: comped trips of your own to appraise hotels, resorts, and restaurants for prospective clients.

Pay range: Annual salaries can run around $56,000, according to PayScale.com. Hourly wages range from $10.93 to $22.16.

Qualifications: Community colleges often offer technical training and continuing education classes for agents. Coursework covers the ins and outs of computer reservations systems, marketing, and regulations for international travel. A few colleges offer full degrees in travel and tourism.

The Travel Institute (thetravelinstitute.com) offers training and professional certifications. The International Air Transport Association (iata.org) has a program for "travel and tourism professional" as well as "consultant." The Cruise Lines International Association (cruising.org), meanwhile, offers its own certifications.

Project Architect

The nitty-gritty: You'll meet with clients to determine objectives and requirements for structures. Give preliminary estimates on cost and construction time. Prepare structure specifications. Direct workers who prepare drawings and documents. Prepare scaled drawings, either with computer software or by hand. Prepare contract documents for building contractors. Manage construction contracts. Visit worksites to ensure that construction adheres to architectural plans. Seek new work by marketing and giving presentations.

In some cases, architects provide predesign services, such as feasibility and environmental impact studies, site selection, cost analyses, and design requirements. Architects may also help clients get construction bids, select contractors, and negotiate construction contracts. Employment of architects is projected to grow 8 percent from 2018 to 2028, faster than the average for all occupations.

Architects are expected to be needed to make plans and designs for the construction and renovation of homes, offices, retail stores, and other structures. Many school districts and universities are expected to build new facilities or renovate existing ones. In addition, demand is expected for more healthcare facilities as the Baby Boomer population ages and as more people use healthcare services.

Demand for architects with a knowledge of "green design," also called sustainable design, is expected to continue. Architects should be needed to design buildings and structures that efficiently use resources, such as energy and water conservation;

reduce waste and pollution; and apply environmentally friendly design, specifications, and materials.

Pay range: The average salary for a project architect is $71,408, according to PayScale. Hourly wages range from $20.47 an hour to over $46.44.

Qualifications: Architects use computer-aided design and drafting (CADD) and building information modeling (BIM) for creating designs and construction drawings. However, hand-drawing skills are still required, especially during the conceptual stages of a project and when an architect is at a construction site.

About two-thirds of states require that architects hold a degree in architecture from one of more than 120 schools of architecture accredited by the National Architectural Accrediting Board (NAAB.org). State licensing requirements can be found at the National Council of Architectural Registration Boards (NCARB.org).

All states and the District of Columbia require architects to be licensed. Licensing requirements typically include completing a degree program in architecture, gaining relevant experience through a paid internship, and passing the Architect Registration Examination.

Aging in Place/Home Modification Pro

The nitty-gritty: Your specialty is to create or rehab a home that will serve long term for people who want to age in place without moving to an assisted-care facility. A mixture of experts can get into the act, from contractors to architects and interior designers. The key is to figure ways to imaginatively convert or adapt homes with lighting, ramps, grab bars in the shower, and more to prevent accidents.

Pay range: $40 per hour and up.

Qualifications: The National Association of Home Builders (NAHB.org), for example, offers a Certified Aging-in-Place Specialist (CAPS) designation that teaches design and building techniques for making a home accessible to all ages.

Publicist/Public Relations Specialist

The nitty-gritty: Getting the word out and burnishing the image of the client you represent is the soul of this remote job. Attention to detail and top-drawer communication skills are your calling cards, and often your network of contents in the media world. You may be generating social media content, supporting advertising campaigns, and writing press releases while cajoling the media representatives who can carry your message to the public. You'll need to be nimble to respond to information requests from the media. It's also possible that you may be asked to write speeches and arrange interviews for a company's top executives.

Pay range: Salaries fall between $48,509 and $63,610, according to Salary.com. That said, education, certifications, additional skills, and the number of years you have spent in your profession can boost that.

The average hourly wage typically falls between $23 and $31.

Qualifications: You'll generally need a bachelor's degree in public relations, journalism, communications, English, or business. This job demands a smooth communication style both written and oral, sharp organization smarts, and an ability to quickly solve problems without a kerfuffle.

Grant/Proposal Writer

The nitty-gritty: You must have a knack for research and be detail-driven. Potential funders generally have precise guidelines that you must follow to apply. Making the case to support a nonprofit or for-profit with a foundation or government grant demands an understanding of the mission of your client's organization and a grasp of the concept or program for which funding is being pursued. You'll need to create a persuasive pitch for why and how the requested funding can make a difference in the outfit's immediate needs and long-term goals and often the world at large. Journalists often shine in this no-nonsense line of remote work.

Pay range: $14.77 to $51.58 per hour and up, according to PayScale. com; part of the compensation may be based on the value of the grant obtained.

Qualifications: A bachelor's degree in communications, journalism, or English is often the baseline. Some jobs may be geared toward those with both experience and a degree or knowledge in a specialized field—for example, engineering or medicine. A familiarity with computer graphics is helpful to tap online technical documentation. The Association of Fundraising Professionals (afpglobal.org) offers several options to obtain certification and a grant proposal writing mini-tutorial on the site. *Grant Writing for Dummies* can help get you started. Many community colleges offer grant-writing certificate programs.

Job hunting tips: Check online job boards like the *Chronicle of Philanthropy* (philanthropy.com/grants) for job postings as well as a data base of grant makers. Job titles: Development Director or Associate, Fundraiser, Grants Manager.

Marketing/Communications Associate or Manager

The nitty-gritty: Duties can range from drafting press releases about upcoming events or capital campaigns to media outreach for coverage in print, broadcast, and social media streams. You might be writing gripping blast emails or mass snail-mail letters. In your public relations role, you may be asked to give speeches, set up speaking engagements, and prepare speeches for the executive director and board members.

Pay range: $48,000 to $88,000, according to PayScale.com. But lots of variables to bump this one up.

Qualifications: A background in media relations, writing, editing, and marketing are the fundamentals. Journalism chops can help. An understanding of a client's particular field—environment, medical, social issues—is best. A gold-standard go-to roster of media contacts is prized. A solid knowledge of social media—Facebook, Google+, Instagram, LinkedIn, Snapchat, Twitter, and other internet platforms—is expected. The American Marketing Association (AMA.org) and Public Relations Society of America (PRSA.org) offer workshops, seminars, webinars, and boot camps on a variety of topics you need to know now, such as social media, green marketing, crisis communication, and branding.

Translator-Interpreter

The nitty-gritty: You may crow that you're fluent in two languages, but are you indeed? It's easy to get rusty. Being a Spanish major back in college isn't going to be adequate. Languages evolve, and being in sync with modern terms and slang is vital. Idioms matter. If you're going to be a Spanish translator or interpreter, for example, you need to know the difference between Spanish spoken in Spain, Mexico, Cuba, Puerto Rico, and different countries in

South and Central America. Note: Interpreters deal with spoken words, translators with written words. Interpreters are the go-between for two parties, such as a doctor and patient, a client and lawyer, and actors or presenters and their audience.

Translation work is generally done on a computer with files transmitted electronically back and forth. Online dictionary resources can be invaluable, but they don't replace expressions gleaned from interacting with others who speak the language frequently. Spanish is the most in-demand language, but other languages are growing, such as Arabic and Mandarin. Specializing in a field such as the judicial system or healthcare and knowing the terminology will increase your job opportunities. This is precise work. Words have consequences. If you don't know the vocabulary, don't take on the task.

Pay range: $11.18 to $39.02 an hour, according to PayScale.com. Depending on assignment and expertise, pay can top $100 an hour. Translation and proofreading projects are generally billed at a rate of 15 to 30 cents per word, depending on the skill level.

Qualifications: Translation careers are an exciting option in remote work. As business is becoming more global, the demand for professionals who can work as translators to bridge the communication gap between cultures and businesses is massive. This is especially important for companies that operate internationally or have operations in other countries where associates must live and work.

Interpreters and translators must be fluent in at least two languages. A subject area of expertise helps. No official certifications are required, although several are offered through trade organizations, such as the American Translators Association (atanet.org), which provides certification in 24 language combinations involving English for its members. Federal courts have certification for Spanish, Navajo, and Haitian Creole interpreters, and many state and municipal courts offer their own forms of certification. The National Association of Judiciary Interpreters and Translators (najit.org) also offers certification for court interpreting. The U.S. Department of State has a three-test series for prospective interpreters. The International Association of Conference Interpreters offers certification for conference interpreters.

If you have solid language skills, you can get translation training at community colleges and universities to prepare you for a translator certification. The American Translators Association has a list of programs it approves, along with a job bank when you're ready. The All Language Alliance (languagealliance.com) also connects job seekers and positions. Internships, apprenticeships, and volunteering via community organizations, hospitals, and sporting events that involve international competitors will build your résumé. The ATA also offers formal mentoring programs and has chapters in many states. Examples of remote translation job titles: Business Translator, Document Proofreader, and Bilingual Writer. After you pass the skills test on Rev.com, you can make between $24 and $39 for each audio hour of transcription.

Hairdresser

The nitty-gritty: This is really a home-based business. An increasing number of established stylists are cutting out the middle man—the salon—and setting up a home studio with a separate entrance. The essence of the job is shampooing, cutting, coloring, and styling. And it goes without saying, it entails a dollop of listening skills. The beauty of it is that you can set flexible hours and can cherry-pick clients.

Pay range: $15 an hour to $25 and up. A typical cut and color, however, can easily top $120 per appointment in many cities. And you might build a side business selling shampoo, conditioners, and other hair products.

Qualifications: All states require hairdressers to be licensed. Qualifications for a license vary by state, but generally a person must have a high school diploma or GED and have graduated from a state-licensed barber or cosmetology school. Some states have reciprocity agreements that allow you to transfer a valid cosmetology license. State licensing board requirements and a list of licensed training schools for cosmetologists may be obtained from the National Accrediting Commission of Cosmetology Arts and Sciences. Background checks are the norm. Good listening skills and stylish flair are your calling cards. Word-of-mouth marketing makes or breaks your success as a hairdresser.

Bookkeeper

The nitty-gritty: Bookkeepers might be in charge of payroll processing to purchasing office, Other responsibilities can include setting up and managing inventory database systems, accounts receivable, and accounts payable. You might be in charge of checking and savings accounts, generating financial reports, chasing down delinquent accounts, and supervising audits and reviews. "With more routinized tasks automated, bookkeepers are expected to take on a more analytical and advisory role over the next 10 years," according to researchers at the Bureau of Labor Statistics. Rather than performing manual data entry, bookkeepers will focus more on analyzing their clients' books and pointing out potential areas for efficiency gains."

Pay range: Generally, $12.08 to $25.34 per hour, according to PayScale.com, but $50 or more is likely, depending on training.

Qualifications: A degree in accounting is desirable; being a CPA is best, of course. But relevant experience or formal training in accounting/auditing services is a plus. Experience with managing a broad range of financial matters for a company, nonprofit, or other organization can qualify you. This skill transfers seamlessly from one industry to another. Other key skills: data entry, and being detail oriented and adept with financial and related computer software. You should be at ease using QuickBooks, or a similar accounting program, used to track and record financial transactions. Solid MS Excel skills are a necessity with most employers.

Job hunting tips: Check out the American Institute of Professional Bookkeepers (aipb.org) for job listings. The group also offers a bookkeeper certification, as does the National Association of Certified Public Bookkeepers (nacpb.org). Community colleges and universities in your area will offer continuing education classes. Employers typically require bookkeeping, accounting, and auditing clerks to have some postsecondary education, particularly coursework in accounting. However, some candidates can be hired with just a high school degree or a GED.

Financial Manager

The nitty-gritty: This job offers a smorgasbord of duties, which keeps it interesting. Your role may be accountant, tax expert, cashier, and more. Duties can run the scope from directing investment activities and producing financial reports to processing payroll checks, managing invoicing, and accounts receivable. Basics such as buying office supplies, monitoring checking and savings accounts, and tracking credit card payments can be part of the landscape.

This job demands a focused, structured approach. Tracking down delinquent accounts can be stressful. Conveying bad financial news to a client entails a steady pragmatic demeanor.

Financial managers work in many industries, including banks and insurance companies. Employment of financial managers is projected to grow 16 percent from 2018 to 2028, much faster than the average for all occupations, according to the Bureau of Labor Statistics. "Several core functions of financial managers, including risk management and cash management, are expected to be in high demand over the next decade," according to the researchers.

Pay range: Median pay is $61.53 per hour, according to the Bureau of Labor Statistics (BLS). More is possible depending on advanced training, degrees, and location.

Qualifications: A degree in accounting or business is generally required. The most common certification is a Certified Public Accountant (CPA). The rigorous exam is administered by the American Institute of Certified Public Accountants. CPAs are licensed to offer a range of accounting services, including tax preparation.

More certifications: A Certified Internal Auditor (CIA) is someone who has passed a four-part test, administered by the Institute of Internal Auditors. The CFA Institute confers the Chartered Financial Analyst (CFA) certification to investment professionals who have at least a bachelor's degree, four years of work experience, and pass three exams. The Association for Financial Professionals bestows the Certified Treasury Professional credential to those who pass an exam and have a minimum of two years of relevant experience.

Other key skills to have in your kit: data entry and being adept with financial and accounting computer software such as QuickBooks (quickbooksonline.com).

Job hunting tips: Network with local business groups, industry associations, or Rotary Club for leads.

Accountant

The nitty-gritty: Duties include preparing financial reports, processing payroll checks, invoicing, and tracking down delinquent accounts. Some firms will ask you to monitor checking and savings accounts and track credit card bills, too. If you have the qualifications, you may be in charge of helping to prepare annual tax returns. Employers run the gamut from start-ups and small businesses to churches and local nonprofits.

Pay range: The U.S. Bureau of Labor Statistics (BLS) reports that the hourly wage for accountants and auditors is between $19.90 and $57.18 and above, depending primarily on experience and industry.

Qualifications: A degree in accounting or business is beneficial, but not mandatory. The most common certification is certified public accountant (CPA). The American Institute of Certified Public Accountants administers the exam. CPAs are licensed to offer a range of accounting services, including tax preparation. Other skills to have in your back pocket: understanding of financial and accounting computer software such as QuickBooks. Familiarity with Word and Excel is expected.

Tax Preparer

The nitty-gritty: To prepare annual income tax returns for individuals or small businesses, you typically will want to be an enrolled agent with the Internal Revenue Service. Your job is to help filers elude penalties, interest, or extra taxes that could result from a going-over by the IRS.

Expect to book copious hours between January and the April tax deadline, particularly if you sign up with a tax preparation firm.

Pay range: $15.76 to $21.00 per hour, according to Indeed.com. Higher wages are possible, depending on the client.

Qualifications: A degree in accounting is helpful, but not required. Computer use is mandatory. You are required to use IRS e-file if you prepare 11 or more returns. Under IRS rules, any individual who, for compensation, prepares or assists in the preparation of a tax return or claim for refund must have his or her own Preparer Tax Identification Number. Check with the IRS (irs.gov) for more guidance. Next, you must pass a competency exam—mandatory for most, but some certified public accountants and others are exempted—to become an IRS registered tax return preparer. Additionally, you must take continuing education courses.

Job hunting tips: Large tax firms—for example, H&R Block and Jackson Hewitt Tax Service—hire thousands of tax preparers annually to join the team from January until May 1. You generally need to take the firm's income tax course in the fall to prepare. You apply via individual stores, but may be able to work remotely. Refresher courses are offered each year. You might start by volunteering with the AARP Foundation Tax-Aide Program (aarp.org/taxaide). It can offer good experience for those who want to graduate to a paying job.

Job-hunting tips: Large financial institutions like Ally Financial, Citi, and Wells Fargo regularly recruit for remote jobs in accounting and finance. Postings include openings for accountants, bookkeepers, and auditors.

Operations Manager or Assistant

The nitty-gritty: Operations jobs involve supervision of workers, materials, services, manufacturing, and business systems to keep a business humming at peak efficiency. Your job is to maximize operating profits. It's all in the ordinary details. You've got to have a keen sense of work flow and an expertise in financial management and systems analysis. If you're seeking an operations position, explore job titles such as Business Operations Manager, Systems Analyst, Inventory Specialist, Operations Officer, Operations Coordinator, and Quality and Process Control Officer.

Pay range: The average operations manager salary in the United States is $97,873, but the range typically falls between $85,162 and $114,426, according to Salary.com. Salary ranges can vary widely depending on many important factors, including education, certifications, and additional skills. The average hourly wage for an Operations Manager ranges between $41 and $55.

Qualifications: Bachelor's degree in business or related field typically required. May require MS Office aptitude.

Financial Planner

The nitty-gritty: There is a growing demand for experts who can help people of all ages manage their money, particularly older adults.

A good planner can devise an overall financial plan that will recommend how to allocate assets and determine if someone has the right blend to meet his or her particular goals.

What's more, a planner advises on how to draw down funds from accounts when needed and handle estate-planning and tax matters. It's a trust relationship, so it can take some building and slow steps. There are also money management jobs that aren't as full-blown as a planner. Consider starting a home-based job-paying or budgeting service that helps people track their monthly inflow and outflow and make sure payments are timely.

Pay range: $120 to $300 per hour, or a percentage of assets under management, generally 1 percent to 3 percent. $10 to $50 an hour for daily and monthly bill and budget aides.

Qualifications: There are myriad designations, from certified financial planner to fee-only planner. As a rule, an adviser should have the Certified Financial Planner (CFP) designation awarded by the nonprofit Certified Financial Planner Board of Standards, Inc. Anyone can call themselves a financial planner or adviser. No minimum experience or education is required by law.

That said, take the time to prepare properly. To learn more about the training necessary, visit the Certified Financial Planner Board of Standards at cfp.net. The CFP designation is a professional certification mark for financial planners conferred by the Certified Financial Planner Board of Standards, Inc. Substantial coursework and a comprehensive, 10-hour exam are required to achieve this title. In general, you'll need a bachelor's degree or its equivalent in any discipline, from an accredited college or university. If you already have an Association of Chartered Certified Accountants (ACCA) or Certified Public Accountants (CPA) credential, for example, you can register for and take the exam without having to complete the education requirements.

You must keep current with the annual certification fee and complete the continuing education (CE) requirement every two years. You can also do a search on the websites of the Financial Planning Association (onefpa.org), the Garrett Planning Network (garrettplanningnetwork.com), and the National Association of Personal Financial Advisors (napfa.org). Another excellent source is the Association for Financial Counseling and Planning Education (AFCPE.org) website.

Website/Platform Designer/Technician

The nitty-gritty: Web designers are innovative with a creative élan, but their toolbox is technical knack to design websites for personal and business use. A web designer creates and codes web pages and related apps for individuals, companies, and nonprofits. You may be hired to revamp an existing site and develop user-friendly and seamless interfaces for employees and customers. You deliver technical and graphical facets of the website or app. In some jobs, you're in charge of keeping the website up to date on a regular basis. Rapid changes in technology require you to constantly stay abreast of the latest bells and whistles. You create applications like a retail checkout tool or write software code. Your creative side may be called on to design the layout of the website and incorporate audio, graphics, and video. The job might entail monitoring website traffic, answering comments, updating content, and fixing broken links.

One popular job title: Front-End Developer. Front-end developers code the front end of a website by converting design files into HTML, JavaScript, or CSS. The online nature of this role makes it one of the best remote jobs to do from any location.

Pay range: The median web designer salary is $49,636 according to Payscale.com, but can range above $74,000. Hourly rate up to $46.12 per hour.

Qualifications: Computer programming and coding language skills must be second nature to you. Calm problem solving is imperative as well. Deadline pressure can be constant, so time is of the essence. People skills and communication finesse will serve you well in dealing with anxious and sometimes demanding clients. Most web designers have an associate's or undergraduate degree in computer programming or a related field. Some have graduate degrees in a related field as well. Designers often have a background in graphic art or visual design. And a potential employer will certainly want to review your website design and development portfolio. Jobs postings typically list required skills in Adobe Creative Suite and design fundamentals using HTML, CSS, and JavaScript, as well as familiarity with content management systems (CMSs) such as Drupal, ExpressionEngine, WordPress, and Sketch. For some possible leads, flexjobs.com/jobs/telecommuting-Website-jobs has a glut of listings. Many, however, are contract positions.

Leslie Bailey-Clarke
Account Manager

Leslie Bailey-Clarke, 55, lives in Covington, Georgia, works remotely as a commercial lines account manager for a provider of insurance and risk management resources based in Texas, and is also a voice coach. She started working in the insurance industry as a customer service rep right out of college. Now, after forays into insurance sales and management, she's back in a customer service-oriented job, working out of a guest-room-turned-office in her home. The impetus for her transition to home-based work, she says, is: "I wanted to spend more time with my teenage daughter."

What she does: "I work a 20-hour week. I generally start at 8 a.m. and work until 4 p.m. three or four days a week. It's so flexible they leave it to me. I tell them on Friday what I'm going to do for the week following, say, 8 to 4 one day, maybe 8 to 12 another day, maybe 1 to 4 on another."

"I start my day with coffee and bring my breakfast tray up to my office to begin checking emails and clock in. I don't usually get out of my sweat pants and T-shirt until lunch time."

Bailey-Clarke works with her client's existing customers, providing proof of insurance on their behalf, getting them new rate quotes at renewal time, and renewing their existing contracts.

The crux of the job is email, email, email. "I communicate by email pretty much the whole day," says Bailey-Clarke, who is an independent contractor and licensed insurance agent. "I can't tell you how much I appreciate the quiet. I usually have some classical jazz music playing quietly."

How she landed the job: "I discovered Work at Home Vintage Experts (WAHVE.com) through an online search. It was a rigorous vetting process, but worth it. Once I was accepted in their database, they matched me with a job that offered the hours I want."

Her challenge: It's a part-time job with no overtime, so that limits how much Bailey-Clarke can make. "Of course, that challenge pushes me to be more diligent in my other income opportunities," she says, "such as the piano and voice lessons that I give out of my home."

What she likes about the job: The flexibility. "If they had been strict, and said you have to work 9 to 5, three days a week," she says, "that probably would have been a deal breaker for me. ... I'm here for my daughter to go to her basketball games and more, and I can travel and still work on the road."

Her income: Bailey-Clarke works around 30 hours a week for $20 an hour. She also devotes several hours a week to providing voice and piano lessons to ambitious actors, public speakers, and performers.

Digital Marketing/Social Media Specialist/Manager

The nitty-gritty: Your primary task is to fire up your employer's following on social media platforms like Facebook, Instagram, LinkedIn, Pinterest, Snapchat, and Twitter. You may also be in charge of fine-tuning the website's design and keeping it well run and accurate. Small-business owners and artists and craftspeople (even authors), lean on a social media presence to attract customers and build a professional brand. Not everyone has the ability or the time to wear this sales hat. That's where you come in. Managing social media can be a time suck and frustrating if you don't know the rules of the road. That's where you step in.

    Some of the fun of managing an online brand—whether it is a person or a business—is choosing what content to feature on social media channels. Duties may include keeping a site fresh by posting timely blogs, or other news content that you ghostwrite or edit for your client. You'll chime in with online discussions and industry news as your boss's alter ego, retweet other people's posts that reflect positively on your client, and swat back spam when necessary. Tracking metrics and engagement are also tasks that fall under your jurisdiction.

Pay range: $37,000 to $89,000 annually, according to Glassdoor.com. Salaries vary widely by location.

Qualifications: Strong writing and communications skills are indispensable. You'll want to be a whiz at generating HTML content and working with software packages such as Adobe Creative Suite (Photoshop and Illustrator) and Microsoft Office. Expertise in tapping social networks is a skill you learn by doing it day in and day out, so you can stay on top of the rapidly changing platforms. You might seek out a local small business in need of a social media presence. You might also launch this one as your own work-from-home business. Initially, you might accept a few clients pro bono to get a referral list for paying customers. For an overview of the major social media sites and to learn the latest ways to use social media as a marketing tool, you might enroll in a community college social media certificate program.

IT Project Manager

The nitty-gritty: Meeting deadlines, holding costs in check, sticking to quality standards, and encouraging a team of other IT professionals, such as computer systems analysts and support specialists, will be fundamental to your success. You're accountable for creating, implementing, and following projects related to IT, software, or web development. You work hand-in-hand with the development team and other departments on each project, such as finance, HR, marketing, and others. Your projects can run from the installation and maintenance of computer hardware and software to conferring with vendors. This job comes in many variations from wide-ranging strategic duties to narrow responsibilities, contingent on the size of the business.

Pay range: $55,000 annually to more than $126,000, according to Payscale.com.

Qualifications: A bachelor's degree in computer or information science, plus related work experience is typically a requirement. Many firms require their computer and information systems managers to have a graduate degree such as a Master of Business Administration (MBA) as well. It helps, though, if your work know-how is in the same industry you're applying to work in. For example, it's a boost for a medical center IT director to have work experience in the healthcare arena. On flexjobs.com/jobs/project-management, for instance, you'll find project management positions that offer remote work options, along with other types of work flexibility, such as freelance contracts, flexible schedules, and part-time work.

Insurance Rater

The nitty-gritty: You'll generally need a background in the insurance industry. The work can be fast-paced and since software is always changing you need to be nimble and curious about ongoing training to keep up to date.

Pay Range: $32,000 to $50,000 or an average hourly rate of $17.15, according to Payscale.com.

Qualifications: A college degree in accounting, business, economics, finance, or a related field may boost job prospects. Insurance-related work experience is key for some positions. Certification is generally necessary for advancement to senior underwriter and underwriter manager positions.

Norma Oquendo
Insurance Rater

For Norma Oquendo, a commercial insurance rater, who lives in Whitsett, North Carolina, continuing to work was a necessity after she lost her job as an operations manager when her employer shuttered its doors. She was 62. "The job search was grueling. Finally, I found that age doesn't matter when you work from home. These insurance agents don't know me. They don't know I'm working from home. All they know is they sent something in. I responded, and they got what they needed."

What she does: Oquendo works 35 hours a week providing insurance-rate quotes to insurance agents for property, casualty, or liability coverage for businesses such as a convenience store, hotel, or a motel.

It's fast-paced work. "We have a 24-hour turnaround to get the rate quote in an agent's hands," she says. "Sometimes I get flooded with 20 quote requests in one day. We have several rating data bases we work with to find the best quotes for our clients. I enter the information from applications, which the agents send to me, into the appropriate database. I check for missing information. One insurance company might like motels, another won't. Based on that knowledge of the industry, I will know what company to rate it with. And after an insurer quotes me a price, I find out whether the customer wants to move forward."

How she landed the job: After her former employer, a small insurance business, closed, Oquendo started searching for independent consulting positions. "I found that as you age, it's more difficult to find a job. No matter how much experience I had, no matter how much excitement or energy I had, none of it mattered because of my age, and that was very frustrating."

So she decided to see if she could find a work-from-home job that was age-blind and where experience mattered. First, she did a hard scan of her marketable skills, and determined that her expertise lay in property and casualty insurance products and services, management, customer relations, policy analysis, problem solving, quality control, and workflow analysis. "It was quite a laundry list," she says. Then she went online and started searching. "I found the work from a placement agency, WAHVE. com. "It was the perfect fit for me. They valued my experience."

The application process took several months, and included an application, some tests, a background check, and an interview.

The challenges: "I miss the interaction with co-workers," Oquendo says. "No paid vacations is a concern. And if you do take a vacation, who is going to do the work you've been doing?"

What she likes about the job: New software is continually being introduced in her business, and Oquendo enjoys learning how to use it. "That's challenging and fun," she says. "You can't be stuck in old ways of doing things." The job also suits her personality. "I'm pretty disciplined and more of an introvert," she says. "I love that I go outside and feel the sun whenever I want a break." She also likes the mobility. If she visits family out of state, she says, "I pack my laptop and take my work with me."

Her income: Oquendo makes $17 an hour.

Quality Assurance Specialist

The nitty-gritty: This is a job for the detail-oriented worker with a sharp eye. You're accountable for making sure software products meet quality compliance regulations and standards through recurring reviews and analysis. You may also be the channel for grouchy customers complaining about complications.

Pay range: $40,000 to $87,000 annually for all fields of quality assurance, according to PayScale.

Qualifications: A bachelor's degree in business administration, management, finance, or industrial engineering can be a prerequisite, but requirements vary by company. An employer may look for those who have a background in their field. Certification is often not required but can't hurt. The ASQ.org (American Society for Quality) offers credentials as a certified reliability engineer, certified quality engineer, and certified quality auditor.

Software Engineer

The nitty-gritty: Software engineers code, design, and develop programs and applications, along with upgrades. The explosion of software, and the need for mobile digital platforms such as tablets and cell phones, have propelled a swelling number of positions, according to the BLS. Cybersecurity is also a growing dynamic in this field as security software plays a crucial part for businesses focused on guarding their computer networks. Industries that employ software developers and engineers run the gamut from computer and electronic manufacturers to software publishers to finance and insurance firms.

Pay range: $65,000 to $125,000 annually, according to PayScale.com.

Qualifications: A background working in software development and engineering is a criterion. In general, a bachelor's degree is required, typically in computer science, software engineering, or mathematics. Software developers should also have a solid working knowledge of the industry in which they work.

Technical Support Specialist

The nitty-gritty: This is one for the calm, cool troubleshooter. Employment of computer support specialists is projected to grow 10 percent from 2018 to 2028, faster than average for all occupations, according to the BLS. Help-desk technicians often work for support service firms that contract with clients that don't have the financial resources to afford their own IT departments.

Pay range: $32,912 to $70,879 annually, according to PayScale. The highest-paid workers, however, earned more than $81,260, according to the BLS.

Qualifications: You may need certifications from a technical school or community college in specialties such as Cisco Networking and Microsoft Access. Employers often will provide on-the-job training about their specific product or service.

Technical Writer

The nitty-gritty: If plainly describing techie topics gets you going, here you go. The rise of high-tech products in the home and the workplace, and the snowballing complexity of medical and scientific information in daily living, are generating openings for technical writers. These jobs come in a variation of flavors—part time, telecommuting, and home-based projects— and range from writing how-to manuals to tutorials and "frequently asked questions" pages. You might also find yourself writing grant applications.

Pay range: The median technical writer annual salary is $74,634 to $114,125, according to Salary.com.

Qualifications: You'll need top-flight writing ability and a hankering for technology and scientific topics. The Society for Technical Communication (stc.org) and other associations offer certification for technical writers. The American Medical Writers Association (amwa.org) offers far-reaching continuing education programs and certificates in medical writing. And some employers provide short-term on-the-job training.

Web Search Evaluator/Search Marketing Specialist

The nitty-gritty: Your work is to play the role of a classic user and rate the quality of the results of a posted internet query, and help clients improve the relevance of their search engine results and performance. This is generally an independent contract, part-time venture—plan on around 20 hours a week. Firms that hire evaluators include Appen and Lionbridge.

Pay range: The average annual salary is $35,471, according to Glassdoor. Hourly pay typically runs $13.50 to $15, although you may be paid per task.

Qualifications: Before hiring, many companies will give you a basic course on their operations and then require you to pass a qualifying exam. You'll need a high-speed internet connection and a computer or mobile device such as an Android phone or iPhone.

Virtual Assistant

The nitty-gritty: With shrinking payrolls, there's been a jump in demand—from small-business operators to executive-level professionals—for virtual personal assistants to do various administrative tasks. Duties range from making travel arrangements to sending letters and other support services such as setting up meetings and appointments, overseeing calendar management, taking meeting notes, organizing digital files, responding to emails, and more. These can all easily be handled remotely via email and phone.

The job can involve sitting for long periods, so take precautions to prevent eyestrain, stress, and repetitive motion ailments such as carpal tunnel syndrome. Look for openings and information at the International Virtual Assistants Association (ivaa.org) and Upwork.com. You can also canvas virtual assistant roles via online job boards. Search for "virtual assistant."

Pay range: $10.13 to $29.99 an hour, according to PayScale. com.

Qualifications: Employers increasingly demand knowledge of computer software applications, such as desktop publishing, project management, spreadsheets, and database management. You should be skilled in both Microsoft Word and Excel (for financial statements). It helps to be up to speed on project management apps such as Basecamp (basecamp.com) and Asana (asana.com), and communication apps such as Slack (slack.com) and Workspace ONE Boxer. Two years of work experience in an office administrative function is helpful. Virtual assistant training programs are available at many community colleges. There is currently no national standard of certification for virtual assistants. Time Etc.

(be-a-virtual-assistant.timeetc.com) is a marketplace for virtual assistants, who can make up to $16 an hour helping clients perform basic administrative work.

Paulette Weems
Virtual Assistant

Paulette Weems, a Miami resident, works as a virtual assistant for a range of clients. She coordinates email communication and sets up Zoom virtual meetings for marketing firms. She helps organize the schedule of an airplane pilot. Other clients have included a mental health professional, an attorney, and the head of a school.

"I call it the minutiae management," says Weems. "We keep those little things at bay, so they can stick to the bigger things."

A lot of tasks start out by helping people get a handle on their calendar and email management. One client, for example, had upward of 45,000 emails for her to sort through, and answer if needed.

Weems generally works between 30 and 35 hours a week. And the time per client varies, although it typically averages between 10 and 15 hours a week. "It's really up to you what your happy place is going to be, but the idea is not to go over 40 hours a week."

Her past experience as the executive assistant to the chief of police at the Miami Gardens Police Department and nearly 25 years spent working at the Hialeah Police Department as a payroll clerk and training coordinator made her a good fit for the job. Her previous work experience included day-to-day administrative support, and responding to requests for information from the public, law enforcement agencies, and the media.

She transcribed dictation, composed and typed correspondence, and proofread incoming and outgoing correspondence for grammatical accuracy, content, and format. She was also in charge of managing executive leadership schedules, including arranging appointments, maintaining electronic calendars, making travel arrangements, and developing itineraries.

But she still had to ramp up her skills for her new post as a virtual assistant by going online with Lynda.com (now LinkedIn Learning) to refresh her Excel skills and learn the project management software Asana and Basecamp. "That was a little form of intimidation for me. I was probably not as savvy with technology as other applicants were. But I had the communication skills down."

The bulk of her virtual assistant duties are done by email and communication apps such as Boxer, Slack, and Zoom. But, of course, "the average client you want to meet with at least once a week by phone," she says.

To avoid getting sucked in by her work, Weems sets a schedule, typically 8 a.m. to 6 p.m. Eastern time, but since clients may be in different time zones, there is fluidity in between, she says.

How she landed the job: Amid a change in administration, Weems lost her job as an executive assistant to the chief of police at the Miami Gardens Police

Department, where she had worked for over eight years. She wasn't quite sure what she'd do, but she knew she wanted and needed to continue working. "I had not had to apply for a job for 20- some years. Just the task of putting together a résumé was pretty crazy."

Weems spent about five months trolling the major job boards looking for administrative and clerical positions. "I applied for probably around 243 jobs," she says. "Out of all of those, I actually got three phone interviews and two in-person interviews. I was getting so depressed. It was ridiculous."

Then a posting for executive virtual assistants at Belay Solutions (BelaySolutions.com) popped up on the job board Flexjobs.com, and Weems was curious. She began investigating the company, and reading online reviews. She filled out the application, hired a résumé writer specializing in résumés for work-at-home job seekers, and sent off a résumé. And she got invited to participate in two face-to-face interviews with a hiring manager via Zoom conferencing. Two months later, she had landed her first job. "They match you with your clients, and they vet the companies."

What she likes: There's plenty of sunshine in her home office, and she has time for family. "The decrease in stress levels is unbelievable," says Weems.

The challenges: Friends and family can be disruptive. "They know you are working from home, but they still call during the workday. They stop by to visit. I have to constantly remind them, 'I'm working. Yes, I am home. Yes, I am wearing yoga pants. But I am working.'"

Her income: Weems, who works about 35 hours a week, made approximately $35,000 last year.

Digital Operations Manager

The nitty-gritty: Calling problem solvers who use advanced methods, such as optimization, data mining, statistical analysis, and mathematical modeling, to develop solutions that help businesses and organizations operate more efficiently and cost-effectively, or do research for projects and communicate about each project's status within the operations department, including to executives and program managers. Liaise with other departments and vendors to obtain and update project information or materials. Coordinate project and operations audits, inventories, and shipments. Schedule, track, and provide support materials for meetings and project events.

Pay Range: $13.00 to $24.28 an hour, according to Salary.com.

Qualifications: Some analysts have degrees in other technical or quantitative fields, such as engineering, computer science, analytics, or mathematics or a Master's in Business Administration.

Jim Ratzlaff
Research Analyst

Four years ago, Jim Ratzlaff, a research analyst who lives in Happy Valley, Oregon, retired after a 30-year-career, but retirement didn't last long. First of all, his wife was still on the job running her own Pilates studio and teaching classes. Importantly, "We started to eat through our savings," Ratzlaff says. "Plus, we needed a new car. So I needed to go back to work to make ends meet, plus I wasn't feeling useful anymore."

He landed a job at Evanston, Illinois–based Kaul Sales Partners (KSP), a sales and marketing support firm, running projects using a project management software solution to prioritize, track, manage, and organize data.

For over three decades, Ratzlaff worked as a computer programmer, business analyst, and application development manager for global companies such as Boeing, McDonnell Douglas, Blount International, and Fender Musical Instruments, where he was a programmer. "I have been a guitar player for a long time so that was like being a kid in a candy store."

What he does: "I work remotely about four hours a day from Monday to Friday, but it's flexible. I started as a Digital Marketing Administrator putting together marketing emails and sending them out with email software. KSP executes marketing campaigns for our clients, and I research leads for the campaigns. I also do a bit of writing for the campaigns.

"Another part of the job is a little bit of project management to identify software available to use for project management and, once purchased, to configure it and set up how we would use it. I train other people in the company how to use it. Also, when we have a new piece of software, I'll go in and document how to use it. So there's a good variety of work, but it all involves applications and processes."

How he landed the job: "I signed up for one month with FlexJobs, a job site that has work-from-home, flexible, part-time, and freelance work. The hardest part was narrowing my search to what I wanted to do. After that, it took about a week to find Kaul Sales Partners. When they were interested in me, I set up a Zoom interview with them. I had done telephone interviews before but not video."

The challenges: "As an independent contractor, there are no insurance benefits, but I'm on Medicare. Since I work remotely, there's no company picnic, but I don't really miss that sort of thing."

What he likes about the job: "I enjoy managing and organizing data, and troubleshooting discrepancies. I get to work on a variety of things that fall within my skillset: working with applications, research, and writing.

"I love when I have tasks that are consistent with my skillset, such as using computer applications, doing analysis, and the research and writing based on analysis I have done. And given my flexible schedule, I bike probably two or three times a week.

"I like working from home because I don't have to dress up for work and I don't necessarily have to shave. I generally wear shorts and a T-shirt. (Of course, I do have to be sure I have a shirt on if we are doing a video conference.)

"Plus, I like the flexible hours. I don't have to drive to work at a ridiculous time. I get to be with my two golden retrievers, who like to hang out under my desk in our family room. They check on me and go in and out. If I want to take a break, make a cup of coffee, get a snack, walk the dogs, I do it.

"I communicate with my co-workers through Slack messaging software, and we have video meetings on Zoom, so I don't feel out of touch with the team."

His income: Ratzlaff earns roughly $16,000 annually.

Online Teacher or Tutor

The nitty-gritty: Online tutoring is in demand for a range of students, from elementary school straight through adult learners. The subjects most in demand are history, science, math, and English. Foreign language specialties are also seeing an uptick. And there is always a need for help with preparation for standardized tests such as the SAT, GED, and GRE.

An online employer like Tutor.com, which offers one-on-one help to students, is set up so that when a student needs assistance with homework, he or she enters a grade level and subject (such as algebra or AP Chemistry) into the computer log-on screen. The appropriate tutor (the firm has more than 3,000, including certified teachers, college professors, graduate students, and professionals with master's degrees, PhDs, and Ivy League credentials) connects to the student inside the secure online classroom. The student and tutor can chat using instant messaging, draw problems on an interactive whiteboard, share a file to review essays and papers, and browse resources on the web together. With individual accounts, sessions are saved so that students and parents can review them at any time. Course levels range from elementary school through twelfth grade and the first year of college, but tutors also can help adults returning to school or searching for a job.

Other online tutoring firms include Wyzant (wyzant.com), which tutors people in more than 300 subjects from accounting to physics to writing. Many of Wyzant's 80,000 tutors are, or have been, teachers or have advanced degrees. Outschool (outschool.com), which offers 10,000 video-assisted classes from preschool through high school, hires instructors who don't need teaching certification, but rather based an individual's work expertise; it pays up to $40 an hour.

But if you have a skill you can pass along, you may be in demand. Prospective tutors complete a proficiency exam for certain subjects, or provide written qualifications. Kaplan and Pearson Education are two more firms to consider.

For general information about tutoring, visit the American Tutoring Association (americantutoringassociation.org/) or National Tutoring Association (ntatutor.com) websites. Or you might opt to tutor on your own. You'll probably forgo the bells and whistles of the interactive whiteboard, but you can easily set up chat sessions and send files back and forth with your students. And you can develop an ongoing relationship that provides steady work. Some firms ask you to plan on at least five hours a week.

Pay range: Hourly rates are all over the map, based on experience, subject tutored, company, and grade level. On Wyzant, an SAT math tutor might charge anywhere from $30 to $200 an hour. And the site will charge you a flat 25 percent platform fee on that sum. Some tutors might charge as little as $15 per hour for their services, while others charge as much as $160 per hour. Online tutors generally earn around $15.13 to $20.26 an hour, according to PayScale.com. Some private tutors, however, can easily make as much as $65 an hour. Annual salaries can top $42,000.

Qualifications: Teacher certification is preferred but not required. Professional experience can be your calling card. A background in education and experience working with students in a classroom is generally a necessity. Teachers should have a bachelor's degree and a valid teaching certificate for the state in which they are teaching and be certified in their grade levels and subject. Many online teachers also have a master's or other advanced degree.

In general, with a tutoring company, you take an online exam in the subject you wish to teach. If you pass, you will be given a mock session with an online tutor. Then you must pass a third-party background check and final exam. Knowledge of more than one subject is encouraged. Your computer must have high-speed internet access and be able to run the classroom software provided.

There is no certification to be a private tutor. Experts in a range of fields from nursing to finance to law and business may find opportunities, as can those with foreign language skills. If you're interested in becoming a college admissions counselor, you can learn more about how to prepare from the Independent Educational Consultants Association (IECAonline.com) and Higher Educational Consultants Association (HECAonline.com). You can get paid $20 an hour to be a tutor at Chegg (chegg.com/tutors/become-a-tutor) or teach a class on Skillshare (skillshare.com) for a price you set.

Job hunting tips: Math teachers are in particular demand at the high school level. Requires a BA/BS degree, technical skills, and a teaching license.

Diana Hood
Teacher

Diana Hood runs a virtual classroom for Connections Academy, a tuition-free online public school for students in grades K–12, reaching 200-plus high school students. There are no chalky blackboards, or marked-up white boards, or shiny apples on the desk.

Hood worked as an English teacher and school librarian for 33 years at various school districts in Texas. Seven years ago, she qualified for retirement through the State of Texas, and decided to take advantage of this to spend more time and travel with her husband. But when the marriage fell apart two years later, she realized that she wasn't completely ready to hang up her lesson plans.

Today, her remote classroom is what was once her now-grown daughter's bedroom. It is a mixed-use room lined with books, her desk, a computer and printer on one side, and her sewing machine and an armoire filled with her cake decorating supplies on the other for her hobbies.

Her school day begins at 8 a.m., after she has taken Zoe, her border collie, for a neighborhood walk around her Leander, Texas, neighborhood. The day wraps at 4 p.m. "Zoe comes over and starts nudging me, kind of saying, 'Hey, get up, get up!'" she says.

Each day is a little different. "The first hour I go through emails from kids," she said. "I might do some grading. There might be a faculty meeting or school meeting at 8. Around 10 you start hearing from kids as they start waking up and logging on themselves. They call me, or I might have a list of calls to return. Sometimes they call after-hours and leave a voice mail."

Hood sets aside late morning or early afternoon for personal tutoring sessions, followed by a class session that she preps for just like a classroom. "We record each class and post the link on a message board for kids who can't be there.

While roughly 200 students can access her classroom, she has 30 students in her home room. Hood's 10-month schedule follows the Texas public school schedule with the same holidays.

And she can connect with colleagues. "I'm on a team with four senior English teachers," she said. "We use Google Hangouts and instant messenger, so we can chat with each other throughout the days, or we can call."

In Austin, she connects with numerous online teachers for coffee or adult beverages after school.

What she does: "I teach English to high school seniors. During the course of the year, the students read excerpts from *Beowulf, The Canterbury Tales, Macbeth*, or other Shakespeare works. It's a traditional British literature class and is considered to be fairly rigorous and college prep. Students do a lot of reading, and they write papers, which I grade. They have essay questions on end-of-unit tests, and I grade those. There are some daily grades. The computer grades the multiple-choice tests.

"I make a lot of phone calls. I call kids. I call parents. A lot of kids jump into online schools thinking this is going to be easy, but when they don't have a teacher standing over them saying do this, do this, do this— well, they tend not to do anything. So I spend a lot time calling kids and saying 'Hey, you're falling behind; hey, I see you haven't done this; hey, are you having trouble, do you need my help, do you need to ask a question?'

"We use a program called Adobe Connect, which has a webcam feature so they can see us when we are teaching and tutoring."

How she landed the job: "I heard about the opportunity from former colleagues, did my research, and applied online at the Connections Academy (ConnectionsAcademy.com) website. The interview process is by phone and in person and there are the prerequisite background and credential checks and references. I am certified in Secondary English instruction, reading, and learning resources."

What she likes: "I can talk to kids one on one without worrying about kids going nuts behind me."

The challenges: The physical distance, in some cases. "I can't say, 'Sit in that desk and finish that.' You have to rethink how you motivate kids. You have to learn to be disciplined with your time. That can be an adjustment when you've lived your life from bell to bell."

Her income: Around $50,000 for a 10-month school year, which is on par with the surrounding school districts.

Learning and Development Curriculum Designer

The nitty-gritty: Curriculum or instructional designers write and create academic training and course materials for schools, corporations, and nonprofits aimed at employee learning opportunities.

Education professionals with experience in curriculum writing will find a variety of part-time, temporary positions to assist educational institutions and organizations with curriculum development, writing, and adoption. These jobs seek people who have excellent teamwork skills and who perform well under deadlines.

Duties can include updating and writing syllabi, creating online course content, and using feedback to update course materials. You'll connect with subject matter experts to provide course content and training curriculum. The aim is to work with your clients to create custom training programs to meet their needs. You may also track employee performance and measure training aftermaths.

Pay range: The salary can range from $59,036 to $90,960, with a median salary of $74,893, according to Salary.com.

Qualifications: You will typically need a bachelor's degree. Most positions require a few years of related work experience as a teacher or an instructional leader. For some positions, experience teaching a specific subject or grade level is required. Master's degree programs in curriculum and instruction teach about curriculum design, instructional theory, and collecting and analyzing data. To enter these programs, candidates usually need a bachelor's degree in education. Check with your state's board of education for specific license requirements.

Online ESL Teacher

The nitty-gritty: ESL (English as a Second Language) teachers teach English to non-native students. The number of students in public schools who speak English as a second language is on the rise. Teaching English as a second language, however, demands skills beyond simply having a grasp of grammar. You will need to consider a number of factors before beginning a career in English language teaching. Where do you want to teach? What level do you want to teach? What are your qualifications?

Virtual teachers may meet one on one with students via Zoom, Skype, or Google Hangouts, or in a group setting via a remote connection. Grading student work, keeping attendance sheets, and creating curriculum are commonly part of the duties. You may also help students to understand day-to-day living challenges and customs in the U.S. culture. Your job may cover coursework in other subjects (such as math and science) or even teaching those subjects directly.

Pay range: Pay runs the gamut from $30,000 to $64,000 annually, according to PayScale.com.

Qualifications: As with other teaching jobs, a bachelor's degree with emphasis in education is required, and a master's degree is highly desirable. Because there is such a wide range of ages among ESL students, additional coursework in specific areas such as early childhood education or adult education is also sometimes required. Certification by the specific state in which a teacher will be employed is a must. You might enroll in a 120- to 180-hour course to earn a certificate to teach English as a Second Language for Adults. Check local colleges and universities for programs. TESOL International Association (tesol.org) is a great resource for jobs and certificate programs. Check out the career development section for more.

Market and Survey Researchers

The nitty-gritty: You mingle research and people skills conducting surveys of customers—either on the phone, online, or through questionnaires via email. Typically, you'll be asked to write a comprehensive report and deliver an analysis of your findings. In some instances, you're sizing up prospective sales of a product or service. Other times you're pulling together statistical data on rivals, prices, and more.

The list of possible employers runs the scope from consumer products firms to university research centers to financial services organizations, government agencies, healthcare institutions, and advertising firms. You'll need to be a nitpicker for details, since this kind of work tends to rely on exact data reviews. For information about careers and salaries in market and survey research, contact the Insights Association (insightsassociation.org).

Pay range: Market research analysts in the United States take home an average salary of $53,322 annually, according to PayScale.com. Overall earnings for market research analysts can stretch to $77,000, including bonuses.

Qualifications: A grounding in liberal arts and social science courses—including economics, psychology, and sociology—is valuable. A master's or doctoral degree may be mandatory, especially for more analytical positions. Quantitative skills are expected for some survey research positions, so courses in mathematics, statistics, sampling theory and survey design, and computer science are helpful. An advanced degree in business administration, marketing, statistics, and communications may give you an edge. Having some training in survey research methodology is, of course, advantageous.

THE HOTTEST FIELD FOR REMOTE WORKERS

Job seekers can find a smorgasbord of remote openings in healthcare, especially moving forward with jobs like telehealth nurse, or a nurse clinician who develops materials for educating nursing staff. These positions are sparked by the aging global population. We're living longer and presumably healthier lives. Some of the telecommuting jobs available in the medical and health field are healthcare information specialist, medical transcriptionist, medical coder, medical billing, research scientist, pharmaceutical representative, nursing, physician care, insurance representative, and patient advocate. The possibilities are boundless for medical and health professionals to find remote contract, independent, part-time, and full-time jobs.

Employment of healthcare occupations is projected to grow 14 percent from 2018 to 2028, much faster than the average for all occupations, adding about 1.9 million new jobs, according to the Bureau of Labor Statistics (BLS). Healthcare occupations are projected to add more jobs than any of the other occupational groups. And as the world shifts due to the 2020 coronavirus pandemic, this figure could expand even further.

Stepping into this growing and ever-changing arena, however, may demand new skills to earn a certification or renew a license. Many employers favor applicants who are certified by a standard professional association. You'll find useful details about healthcare jobs in the Department of Labor's Occupational Outlook Handbook (bls.gov/ooh/). Here are some great healthcare jobs to consider.

Dietician and Nutritionist

The nitty-gritty: Employment of dietitians and nutritionists is projected to grow 11 percent from 2018 to 2028, much faster than the average for all occupations, according to the Bureau of Labor Statistics. More dietitians and nutritionists will be needed to provide care and education for patients with various medical conditions and to counsel people who want to improve their overall health.

There's rising demand for special diets to tackle obesity, aging, allergies, and ailments such as diabetes and heart disease. And staying fit and eating healthy are typical life goals, particularly for those over age 50.

Duties range from meal designing to providing expert advice on, for instance, weight loss and lowering cholesterol levels. Potential employers include operators of wellness programs, supermarkets, schools, restaurants, hospitals, clinics, and nursing care facilities. You might opt to open your own practice as a nutrition or health coach. Appointments can be held via telephone or Zoom, Skype, or other video conferencing platform, so you and your client can work together quietly without interruption.

Pay range: The average salary for a registered dietician is $52,062, but can range up to $68,000, according to PayScale.com, or $20.53 to $37.75 per hour. Nutritionists can earn up to $72,000, according to PayScale. Depending on your expertise, you might charge $175 for an initial 90-minute consultation. Follow-up sessions are typically 30 to 45 minutes in length and are billed at $65 per half hour.

Qualifications: You'll usually need a state license or certification, which requires a bachelor's degree in food and nutrition, a supervised internship, and a passing grade on an exam. You can get more information from the Academy of Nutrition and Dietetics (eatright.org). Other options include a health coach certification from the American Council on Fitness (acefitness.org) and various certifications offered by the American Fitness Professionals & Associates (afpafitness.com).

Massage Therapist

The nitty-gritty: Massage therapists are valued for their talent for relieving muscle soreness and unknotting stress for their clients. Employment outlooks are on the rise. This is a job well suited to a home-based business where your clients come to your in-house studio, which is equipped with a special table, crisp linens, soothing music, and aromatic balms and lotions of lavender and sage.

Massage therapists use a variety of treatments and techniques, and you may choose to specialize in one. My 90-year-old mother's therapist is known for her work with older adults and a gentle massage aimed at circulation, relaxation, and delivering the human touch. Your core work consists of assessing the client's medical past and delivering what the client seeks, whether that is a gentle or a more aggressive workout.

Pay range: Therapists who have clients come to their homes typically charge between $50 and $125 for a 90-minute massage. Some also make house calls for an extra fee.

Qualifications: Most states and the District of Columbia regulate massage therapy. You must get either a license or certification after graduating from an accredited training program. You may also need to join a massage-professional organization for insurance coverage. The American Massage Therapy Association (amta-massage.org) offers memberships, which include liability insurance, for $235 a year.

Virtual Nurse

The nitty-gritty: A virtual nurse is often referred to as a home health nurse or a telehealth nurse. Nurses use technology like web cameras, VoIP (Voice over Internet Protocol), the internet, and telephone lines to convey care to patients. You might be responsible for conducting post-discharge calls, answering acute care requests, assessing needs, referring callers to healthcare providers, services, and community resources. Nurses working remotely are often in charge of case management, treatment approval, and patient education.

Pay range: Hourly pay can range from $19.11 to upward of $39.44, according to PayScale.com. Annual salaries can top $80,000.

Qualifications: Prerequisites include a nursing degree, a nursing license, and the computer and communication skills essential to deliver health advice over a video call or telephone. Emergency medicine nurses may feed triage services over video links, which requires certification as an emergency medicine nurse. Employers include medical practices, major medical centers, and university hospitals, as well as hospice and home care providers. Employers include: Humana, Aetna, and UnitedHealth Group.

Medical Biller/Coder

The nitty-gritty: The essence of this job is to switch medical terminology for everything from an annual physical exam to a torn ACL into the numerical standard codes using the classification system that insurance companies use for administering reimbursement. Titles for this job include clinical coding officer, diagnostic coder, medical coder, or medical records technician. Potential employers include billing companies, physician offices, hospitals, hospices, clinics, and insurers.

Pay range: Annual salaries can range from $40,249 to upward of $71,697, according to Salary.com.

Qualifications: Plan on four months to one year of education. With an online course, you can go at your own pace. In general, you'll need a high school diploma or GED, and must pass an accredited program in medical coding. Most employers require that you get certified through a nationally recognized professional organization such as the American Academy of Professional Coders (aapc.com) or the American Health Information Management Association (ahima.org).

Medical Interpreter

The nitty-gritty: The Bureau of Labor Statistics projects 19 percent employment growth for interpreters and translators through 2028. Specializing in healthcare expands your opportunities, but you'll need to know quite an assortment of medical terms in both languages. Spanish is the most in-demand language, but the need for Arabic, Chinese/Mandarin, German, Hindi, Korean, Thai, and Russian is growing. Interpreters assist patients in their communications with doctors, nurses, and other medical staff, either face-to-face or remotely by phone or video link. Translators, meanwhile, handle written material such as informational booklets, forms that patients must read and sign, and patient records.

Pay range: The median annual salary for medical interpreters is $45,349, with a range usually from $34,948 to $53,688, according to Salary.com. Top earners can pull in more than $90,000, according to the BLS.

Qualifications: You don't need a college degree, but employers generally prefer to hire certified medical interpreters or certified healthcare interpreters. Some colleges and universities offer certificate programs. To become a medical interpreter, you can complete a 40-hour minimum accredited medical interpreter training course. Find a training program that's accredited by the National Commission for Certifying Agencies (NCCA) and by the Commission for Medical Interpreter Education (CMIE). For example, Howard County Community College in Maryland has a Health Care Interpreter Certificate program that consists of three courses for a total of 124 hours, taking place over five months.

Medical Records Administrator

The nitty-gritty: The work involves transferring records of physician notes from patient visits, medical or surgical procedures, medical history, test results, and more into computerized files. For the most part, this is a stationary desk job. A hot specialty: coding (see above).

Pay range: $12.07 to $23.52 per hour, with annual salaries of $34,000 to above $71,000, according to PayScale.

Qualifications: A high school diploma or equivalent and prior experience in a healthcare setting are enough to qualify for some positions, but most jobs for health information technicians require postsecondary education, according to the BLS. You'll probably need an associate's degree in health information technology from a technical or community college. Online courses are offered, too.

Coursework covers medical terminology, anatomy and physiology, health data requirements and standards, clinical classification and coding systems, healthcare reimbursement methods, and database security.

Passing a certifying examination is not always obligatory, but employers prefer it. This certification is awarded by the American Health Information Management Association (ahima.org). Visit its website for complete information, including accredited schools and certification details.

Healthcare/Patient Advocate

The nitty-gritty: You're in change of helping patients traverse the complex medical system. You can get to the bottom of billing errors and challenge insurance-coverage denials.

At times, you might offer advice in making medical decisions, help locate a specialist or hospital, go with patients to doctor appointments, manage multiple-doctor care, and pick up prescriptions.

Knowing how to fill out insurance forms and even consult with doctors for better rates might fall under your service. Job openings range from working privately and remotely for one person or a couple to working on staff as an advocate at a local hospital, nursing home, rehab center, or insurance company. Some office time might be required.

Pay range: Annual salaries can range from $45,469 to more than $81,000, according to Salary.com.

Qualifications: Community colleges and nonprofit organizations offer training and certification programs to help more people handle this post. Nurses, social workers, medical professionals, and insurance experts are in high demand for these positions. But if you've piloted your own maddening path through the medical system, you might be the ideal person to take on this role. No licenses are required to practice, but there are several credentialing programs. Contact the National Association of Healthcare Advocacy (nahac.com), a professional group in Berkeley, California, and the Patient Advocate Certification Board (pac-board.org).

Medical Writer/Editor

The nitty-gritty: This writing or editing position can range far and wide, from creating documents relating to grant proposals, to writing magazine and newspaper articles and educational booklets, to covering investigational trials, to preparing clinical study reports, poster presentations for medical conferences, summaries of safety and efficacy, and other regulatory deliverables. You'll need a core ability to summarize scientific data, combining a writer's creative flair with the precision of research and the scientific process.

It's a hot field thanks to the relentless innovation in medicine and healthcare. The necessity to communicate about research findings, products, devices, and services is rising. And there's a pressing need to convey new information to healthcare specialists, such as doctors and nurses, as well as patients and the general public. You might find work in traditional print publications, electronic publications, videos, podcasts, website content, and work with doctors and scientists.

Other job titles include Scientific Writer, Technical Writer, Regulatory Writer, HealthCare Marketer, HealthCare Journalist, or Communication Specialist. Remote jobs can be found at pharmaceutical and biotechnology companies, medical device companies, government agencies, medical communication agencies, medical education companies, healthcare professionals associations, academic institutions, medical and healthcare book publishers, trade publications, and more.

Pay range: A salary range for a medical writer is $53,000 to $103,000 annually, according to PayScale.com. For a medical editor, the span is $41,000 to $93,000 and up annually.

Qualifications: You will typically need a bachelor's degree and prior work-related experience in hands-on technical/medical writing experience, often in a pharma/biotech environment. Medical communicators may be writers, editors, healthcare journalists, supervisors, project managers, media relations specialists, educators, and more. At their core, they are exceptionally skilled at gathering, organizing, interpreting, evaluating, and presenting often complex information to healthcare professionals, a public audience, or industry professionals such as hospital purchasers, manufacturers and users of medical devices, pharmaceutical sales representatives, members of the insurance industry, and public policy officials. For information, contact the American Medical Writers Association (AMWA.org). Members can access the group's job board.

Senior Statistical Programmer

The nitty-gritty: This remote job may step you into the realm of statistical programmer for projects and programs for clinical studies. You might be part of figuring the overall strategy for the programming duties on a project, help in managing project budgets, and tracking project performance metrics. You work with software developing customized programming code to generate summary tables, data listings, graphs, and derived datasets, as specified in the statistical analysis plan and programming specifications. You also develop and lead the implementation of data management protocols to support pharma/clinical research projects.

Pay range: Annual salary range is $78,000 to $149,000, according to PayScale.com.

Qualifications: Requires a bachelor's degree or higher, preferably in a scientific or statistical discipline; in lieu of a degree, a comparable combination of education and demonstrated programming experience may get you in the door. Programming experience in SAS or other required software, preferably in a clinical trial environment, may be mandatory.

Principal Biostatistician

The nitty-gritty: Statisticians gather and evaluate data and to solve problems in a range of fields from business and sports to engineering, government, and healthcare. You'll be called on to choose what data you need to collect and the best way to do so via a survey or experiment, for instance. You then do the research via phone or online surveys, and then drill down to interpret the findings.

Statisticians known as biostatisticians or biometricians typically work in pharmaceutical companies, public health agencies, or hospitals. You may design studies to test whether drugs successfully treat diseases or medical conditions. They may also help identify the sources of outbreaks of illnesses in humans and animals. Other job titles: Quantitative Analysts, Market Research Analysts, Data Analysts, or Data Scientists.

Pay Range: $85,000 to $137,000, according to Glassdoor.

Qualifications: Statisticians typically need at least a master's degree in statistics, mathematics, economics, computer science, or another quantitative field. However, a bachelor's degree is sufficient for some entry-level jobs. Research and academic jobs generally require a PhD. A bachelor's degree in statistics typically includes courses in linear algebra, calculus, experimental design, survey methodology, probability, and statistical theory. Coursework in engineering or physical science, for example, may be useful for statisticians working in manufacturing on quality or productivity improvement. A background in biology, chemistry, or health sciences is useful for work testing pharmaceutical or agricultural products. Communication skills come in handy since you'll have to present your ideas and findings to those without your analytic chops.

Junior Data Analyst

The nitty-gritty: Junior Data Analysts translate numbers into plain English. Every business collects data, whether it's sales figures, market research, logistics, or transportation costs. A data analyst's job is to take that data and use it to help companies make better business decisions. For instance, you might be hired to work with an employer's social media content and advertising data from top brands, working with A/B testing (also known as split testing or bucket testing), which is a method of comparing two versions of a webpage or app against each other to determine which one performs better, and reporting and analyses.

Pay Range: The average salary is $55,851, according to Indeed. Annual salaries can top $109,000.

Qualifications: Most management analysts have at least a bachelor's degree. The Certified Management Consultant (CMC) designation may improve job prospects. Learn more at the Institute of Management Consultants (imcusa.org) website. A bachelor's degree is the typical entry-level requirement for management analysts.

Fundraiser

The nitty-gritty: Asking for money is a fine art. The lifeblood of a nonprofit's sustainability is its ability to keep the coffers filled with generous support from donors who believe in the mission and cause of the organization. When you accept this role, you're always reaching out to develop relationships with individual donors and lobby for supporters to make a bequest in their estate plans for funds to go to the nonprofit.

You might be the gracious host for events that draw attention and presumably donations to your cause. You might be in charge of shepherding grant proposal requests to the proper foundations (see grant-writing jobs, p. XX), or of launching phone and direct mail appeals. If you're in search of a sizeable gift, you'll be out of your home office, building rapport over long lunches and get-togethers with potential donors in their offices and at their homes. If you delight in event planning, arranging parties with purpose, so to speak, that can be an energizing part of this job.

Pay range: $34,000 to $81,000, according to PayScale.com; Fundraising Director salary falls between $108,127 and $169,650, according to Salary.com.

Qualifications: A background in public relations, sales, or market research is often expected. One way to sharpen your fundraising skills is to enroll in classes and certification programs offered by the Association of Fundraising Professionals (afpglobal.org) and

Candid (Candid.org). AFP offers webinars and publishes books that help fundraising professionals learn. Some of these AFP books are published in partnership with Wiley. Candid offers free and affordable classes nationwide in classrooms, libraries, and online that cover grant proposal writing and fundraising skills. Many colleges and universities offer courses in fundraising. Planned giving specialists should have an understanding of gift and tax law.

Customer Support Specialist/Representative

The nitty-gritty: Start with an up-to-date computer, a high-speed internet connection, a dedicated landline phone during business hours, a telephone headset, and a noiseless place to work. In general, you'll be fielding incoming calls, taking new orders, and tracing current orders. In some cases, you'll troubleshoot and help out with technical help. Online chat sessions and email may be part of the job. You may need to jump back and forth among numerous computer screen windows at a time. Employers typically provide training sessions.

Customer service is the fifth most common remote job category on the job board FlexJobs (Flexjobs.com). Each of the companies below hired for the most work-from-home customer service jobs over other companies in the job board's database. These companies are a great place to start when looking for a work-from-home customer service job: Amazon, American Express, Apple, BCD Travel, Concentrix, Direct Interactions, The Hartford, Liveops, Sutherland, SYKES, Transcom, TTEC, U-Haul, Vivint Smart Home, and Working Solutions.

Sample job titles for these firms are Customer Service Team Manager, Customer Service Associate, Customer Care Professional, Corporate Travel Consultant, Sales and Service Representative, Retail Sales and Customer Service Advocate, Licensed Life and Health Insurance Sales Specialist, Tech Support and Sales Consultant, Bilingual Healthcare Insurance Agent, Bilingual Customer Service Representative, Roadside Assistance Agent, Event Ticketing, and Sales Associate.

Pay range: $9.89 to $19.05 an hour, according to PayScale.com. Some firms provide health, vision, and dental benefits, or access to group plan rates. Paid vacation and matching 401(k) plans may be a perk, but you'll have to clock in enough hours to be eligible.

Qualifications: The positions have comparatively low barriers to entry: generally a high school diploma, some related work experience, and first-rate communication skills. Experience in a retail store, as a bank teller, or in sales might do. Listening and verbal skills are key. If you communicate through email, good typing, spelling, and grammar skills are crucial. Basic to intermediate computer proficiency is a must. You'll likely be given training with background on the company and its products, the most commonly asked questions. Past experience valued includes technical support or interacting with customers via a retail, sales, or other customer service setting such as a hospitality job. There is a growing demand for bilingual reps, especially Spanish-speaking. Typically, an online test and a phone interview are required. Background, drug, and credit checks are standard.

Direct Sales

The nitty-gritty: Selling for a direct sales firm like Amway, Avon, Cutco, Mary Kay, Pampered Chef, and Tupperware can be profitable, and there are ample opportunities to do so. You market the merchandise directly from your home office via a computer, internet access, and a telephone. But it entails plenty of legwork and some start-up costs for a "starter" kit of training materials and products. You set your work schedule. Earnings are commission-based. With some companies, you can bump up your income by enrolling other salespeople to join your team. You then receive a commission for the items they sell, too.

Contact the Direct Selling Association (dsa.org) for information on any particular direct selling firm. Visit business.ftc.gov for Business Guidance Concerning Multi-Level Marketing. Check with your local Chamber of Commerce, Better Business Bureau, or state attorney general's office to see if there have been complaints about a company in the past.

Pay range: You can earn around $300 to $500 a month part-time, up to $1,000 or more full-time. Compensation systems are commission-based—25 to 40 percent generally. You buy the products wholesale and sell them at retail prices. You can increase your earnings draw by recruiting, training, and mentoring new representatives at some companies.

Qualifications: If you use the product and appreciate how it works yourself, it's easy to make a sales pitch that is authentic. If you're peddling makeup, for example, it helps to have some experience in cosmetics and be capable of assuredly offering beauty and skin care advice. The same holds true with cooking tools: If you're an avid cook, you have some insight to share. And you can't be shy. This job is all about your people skills.

Transcriber

The nitty-gritty: To land this gig, a fast internet connection, a laptop, a foot pedal to stop and start the audio recordings (Marcy Brown uses hot keys on her laptop; see the sidebar below), and noise-canceling headphones are really all you need to get rolling. The core of this job is a love for typing and an ability to type quickly and accurately. Then, too, a knack for grammar, punctuation, spelling, and grammar are essential requirements of the job, and of course, a familiarity with Microsoft Word. Two in-demand areas for jobs: medical transcriptionists who listen to voice recordings that physicians and other healthcare workers make and convert them into written reports, and legal transcriptionists who provide written accounts of court and legal proceedings.

Pay range: Pay may be per line or per word. According to Careerbuilder, the average rate for a transcriptionist is $17.20 an hour. The median hourly wage for a Medical Records Transcriptionist is $22, with a range usually between $19 and $27, according to Salary.com.

Qualifications: Employers typically require applicants to do a sample run with a test audio transcription. Many vocational schools and community colleges offer courses in transcription. Medical transcription programs are typically one-year certificate programs. Coursework in anatomy, medical terminology, and a legal background can smooth the way into court transcription work.

Marcy Brown
Transcriptionist

Marcy Brown, a paralegal who lives in Gravois, Missouri, found work as a transcriptionist a couple of days a week. "I didn't want to work 40 hours a week. It's a great work-from-home (or from anywhere) job," says Brown. "I lov d not having to get out and drive somewhere, getting up when I want to get up, and not having to have work clothes."

Although Brown did have a home office set up in a spare bedroom with a desktop computer, she was more likely to be found sitting on the couch in her living room with her laptop, typing away. "I've worked sitting out on our deck because we live right on the lake and have a gorgeous view," she says. "I have also done my transcribing from the front seat of a car on road trips while traveling on an 8-hour drive from my home in Missouri to visit family in Indiana."

Brown learned to type in high school on a manual typewriter. She took three years of typing and two years of shorthand. "I have always liked to type, and the work is interesting. You learn about so many different things. It's fun."

How it worked: The audio files were either emailed to her or sent to a drop box on her computer. Some jobs paid better than others. "My best-paying jobs were deposition transcripts that I typed for a court reporter I worked for. The pay was per page with 25 lines per page. The volume on the recording is usually good. It's easy proofing. I simply did a spell check and then sent it back to the court reporter, who final-proofedit. For those jobs, I could generally make $15 to $20 an hour."

Her other job, which was general transcription, paid .75/audio minute. "I've typed marketing focus group reports, college lectures, interviews conducted for college theses, World War II veteran oral history, book ideas, conference presentations, and more. Some jobs were one-on-one interviews, which I requested usually, but sometimes I'd get jobs with multiple speakers. If they're talking over each other, it made the transcription slower, and reduced the money I could earn hourly."

"I have done a lot of files about STEM [science, technology, engineering, and math], which I really didn't know what it was until I started doing those," says Brown. "I do now. That can slow you down a little bit, but to make transcripts of value, you need to do that extra step. It also requires more detailed proofing, which takes more time and, in turn, reduces my hourly rate."

How she landed the job: Brown landed her first job via a job posting on Craigslist for two court reporters in the Kansas City area, where she and her husband were living at the time. "I sent in my résumé. I met with them, and off I went," she says.

Brown has also found work via the job site Flexjobs.com. She responded to postings, sent a résumé, and transcribed a few sample audio recordings, and sent them back to them to see how she did. At one point, she was juggling four clients.

The challenges: "You have to be a good typist, have a good vocabulary, and be able to spell well. Obviously, there's spell check, but you have to know the difference between their and there."

The court transcription work is a natural given Brown's background, but with the general transcription work it can be a little dicier. "You never really know what you are getting with the general transcription," she says.

Sometimes, it's "Oh my gosh, I don't understand anything they are talking about," and if it's someone with an accent, that can be even harder."

Plus, Brown says, "You have to be able to do a little bit of internet research. A lot of times you are dealing with subject matters that you are completely unfamiliar with. There is terminology in there that you may not know or know how to spell."

When that happened, Brown stopped and did an internet search of, say, a person, a company, or a subject matter, so she could familiarize herself with what she was typing. "That can slow you down a little bit, but to make a transcript of value, you need to do that extra step."

Mediator

The nitty-gritty: Arbitration and alternative dispute resolution (ADR) have steadily gained fans from those hoping to avoid lawsuits with burdensome fees and often a drawn-out legal procedure. From divorce proceedings to housing and medical disagreements, many people prefer to settle matters confidentially out of court. There can be frustrating debates, but mediators are the pros armed with the cool voice of reason.

These jobs are not only for retired lawyers, mind you. An expertise in certain fields of business can be your calling card. Experience settling workplace discrimination issues, marriage counseling, and even a mental health capability can land you a seat at the table to guide a delicate negotiation. In general, you work out of your home office, but you may have to go to another location for the official meeting. You've got to be "all ears." Your task: Neutrally hear both sides of an argument, cut through the occasional emotional drama, and focus on the critical details. It's up to you to patiently direct and encourage both sides to keep talking in a civil fashion until a satisfactory resolution, or settlement, is landed.

Pay range: $137.00 to $381.70 per hour, according to PayScale.com.

Qualifications: Many mediators have law degrees. Specific training, license requirements, and certification vary by state. Mediators typically complete 60 hours of courses through independent programs or organizations, but some are trained on the job through volunteering at a community mediation center or teaming up with a practicing mediator. Some colleges offer certificates or advanced degrees in dispute resolution. To tap into cases, network with local bar associations, insurers, realtors, and human resource departments at area businesses and hospitals. The American Bar Association Section for Dispute Resolution (americanbar.org) provides a trove of information relating to the dispute resolution field. Mediate.com is another source for international, national, and state conflict resolution organizations and more.

Sustainability Building Consultant

The nitty-gritty: In general, a background in architecture, engineering, and construction will give you a firm foundation. Older buildings, in particular, are getting serious facelifts. You probably need a grasp of (or a yearning to learn) the technical aspects of building construction—say, the nature of sieve-like windows, the best ways to use natural lighting, energy-efficient heating and air-conditioning systems (HVAC), plus water-smart features such as low-pressure faucets and toilets.

You'll work with companies to help them to become more environmentally hip. On one hand, they may want to do good, so they're admired in their community, or perhaps you can help them save money by wise management of resources that's good for the bottom line and for the environment.

A sustainability consultant will offer solutions for greener work supplies, ways to apply temperature control, or lighting systems within factories and offices that save energy. You may even be able to help the company qualify for tax credit incentives.

Pay range: Salaries can run from $50,000 to $90,000, according to PayScale.com.

Qualifications: One biggie: The LEED program (Leadership in Energy and Environmental Design; usgbc.org/leed) offers certification that leads to a credential as a green building specialist. That's your entrée to offer strategic advice on a wide range of building projects. The Green Building Certification Institute provides information, as does its parent organization, the U.S. Green Building Council. Generally speaking, you'll have a degree in environmental science and/ or business regulation. While this can be a remote job, you will spend time on site at various operations.

PART II

GREAT COMPANIES FOR REMOTE WORKERS

The key to having a successful remote job is working for an employer who is committed to making it, well, work. With the help of my friends at Flexjobs.com, here are a selection of employers who offer work-from-home jobs and provide the support to make it a win all around. Globally, many employers and employees have adapted to remote working during the 2020 stay-at-home mandates. Moving forward, the option is likely to be embraced by a myriad of companies that were reluctant to offer it in the past. They have found it works. That said, the firms I am spotlighting here are ones that have been forward-thinking and ahead of the trend.

It's not just U.S. companies that are opening up their arms to remote workers, it's a global movement. Global employers are seeking employees across the world, regardless of where they are based. The opportunity of working from anywhere around the world is on the rise and is without question one of the biggest workplace trends of our time.

FlexJobs scrutinized its database of over 54,000 companies and selected the "remote-friendly" ones that post the most remote jobs across an array of professional occupations. "Remote-friendly" means the openings must offer some level of remote work (the levels are "100% remote work," "partial remote work," or "option for remote work").

I've cherry-picked 40 companies from the database of FlexJobs research to give you a sampler of what's out there. Overall, these companies represent more than 15 industries and are headquartered across nearly a dozen different countries. In my expert opinion, this is a valuable one-of-a-kind resource list of potential employers to launch your remote job hunt. For the full listing of 100 employers, please go to Flexjobs.com.

Health and tech-related career fields continue to hold a strong position when it comes to remote jobs, with computer and IT ranking number two for the top career fields for remote work. Those jobs include titles like IT analyst, WordPress developer, consumer application architect, and software engineer.

Jobseekers, I recommend that you identify a company you'd love to work for, whose mission you believe in, and then drill down to the potential jobs they might have available that suit your talents. And then do the digging to see who you know who works there who might be able help you get in the door for an interview.

C H A P T E R

Great Remote Employers

Let's get started with a look at 40 employers who love remote workers.

ADP

Website: adp.com
Headquarters: Roseland, New Jersey
Industry: HR and recruiting
Remote jobs: recruiter, sales, bilingual advisor

About ADP

ADP, founded in 1949, is one of the world's largest providers of business outsourcing. In the past, ADP has offered flexible schedule and remote job opportunities in the HR and recruiting industry, including full-time, 100 percent remote jobs and on-site, part-time jobs. ADP offers a wide range of human resource, payroll, talent management, tax, and benefits administration solutions from a single source and helps clients comply with regulatory and legislative changes.

Past Flexible Jobs at ADP
Client Experience Analyst

Seeking a client analyst to manage projects, build implementation, and solve issues. Must have a bachelor's degree and two-plus years' experience in a similar position. Competitive salary and benefits. Partially remote with some travel.

HR Relationship Manager

Will work on coordinating client projects, promoting client participation in focus groups, promoting key initiatives, identifying new service/product opportunities, and performing strategic account reviews. Full-time, work at home, with 10 to 20 percent travel.

Aetna

Website: aetna.com
Headquarters: Hartford, Connecticut
Industry: Healthcare
Remote jobs: outreach coordinator, content quality reviewer, network relations manager, health coach

About Aetna

Aetna is one of the nation's premier healthcare benefits companies, providing high-quality healthcare and protecting consumers financially from health-related risks. Aetna employs nearly 50,000 professionals and offers a comprehensive benefits package to eligible employees, which may include professional development opportunities, paid time off, access to on-site fitness centers at more than 20 of its locations, community involvement programs, tuition reimbursement, and financial wellness programs. In the past, Aetna has offered part-time, occasional, flexible schedules, and remote jobs in consulting, insurance, and medical and health fields, such as nursing and case management.

Past Flexible Jobs at Aetna
Case Manager RN

Case manager RN needed for a full-time opportunity. This position offers options for remote work and involves travel. Will be responsible for conducting assessments and resolving member issues. RN license and three years' experience required.

Senior Analyst
Full-time position. Will analyze plan requests, review data sets, resolve issues, mentor staff, and perform code reviews. Bachelor's degree and 5-plus years' related experience required. Remote option. Travel.

Amazon

Website: amazon.com
Headquarters: Seattle, Wash.
Industry: Retail, computer and IT
Remote jobs: account management, customer service, and retail

About Amazon
Headquartered in Seattle, Washington, Amazon is the largest online retailer in the world. Through its online marketplace, it offers traditional and e-books, furniture, household items, apparel, electronics, music, movies, and a vast selection of other products. Amazon employs nearly 92,000 employees around the world. The company has offered part-time, seasonal, and remote job opportunities in the past. Amazon maintains a work-from-home program designed to cater to international candidates eager and qualified to work remotely. Past jobs also include opportunities in account management, customer service, and retail.

Past Flexible Jobs at Amazon
Software Development Manager
Software development manager needed for a remote, full-time opportunity. The ideal candidate will have a bachelor's degree in computer science or a related field, five-plus years' experience in software development, and three-plus years' open source experience.

Data Associate
Data Associate is needed for a remote opportunity. Candidate will work with text, speech, and other types of data and attach tags to the contents. Must have proficient computer skills. HS diploma and prior related experience required.

American Express

Website: americanexpress.com
Headquarters: New York, New York
Industry: Accounting and finance
Remote jobs: business analyst, customer care, account development

About American Express

Advocates for flexible work options, American Express attributes its success to remote flexibility, which enables it to cast a wide net to reach prospective employees well beyond its physical locations, as well as be available for customers across time zones. The company has offered temporary, part-time, and remote, work-from-home job opportunities in the past. As a global provider of financial goods and services, American Express delivers solutions related to payment, travel, and financial management for individual consumers and for businesses.

Past Flexible Jobs at American Express
Director Account Development
Seeking an executive director for a remote position. He or she will provide strategic recommendations and solutions to assist clients in optimizing their travel and expense management. At least five years' relevant experience is required.

Virtual Travel Consultant
Full-time, remote position. Must be available to work night and/or weekend hours. Responsibilities include researching, planning, and executing customized travel experiences, de-escalating customer issues, and providing excellent customer service.

Appen

Website: Appen.com
Headquarters: Chatswood, New South Wales, Australia
Industry: Technology (machine learning and artificial intelligence)
Remote jobs: voice coach, linguist, web search evaluator, transcriber

About Appen

Appen is a technology services company that offers jobs across several industries in 130 countries worldwide. Appen employs over 400 professionals and supports nearly a million global contractors. Flexible roles entail working from home anywhere from 5 to 40 hours per week, depending on the project.

Past flexible jobs at Appen
Mandarin Linguist

Needs a bachelor's degree, experience in phonemic transcription of Mandarin, and native speaker of Mandarin. Review guidelines for speech projects involving text processing and audio data evaluation, review inventory. Full-time, 100 percent remote job.

Social Media Evaluator

Remote, part-time position with flexible scheduling. Will provide feedback on newsfeeds, search results, and advertisements. The ideal candidate will reside in and be legally permitted to work in Great Britain and will be an active social media user. Part-time, 100 percent remote job, UK.

BCD Travel

Website: bcdtravel.com
Headquarters: Utrecht, Netherlands
Industry: Travel and hospitality
Remote jobs: travel consultant, accountant

About BDC Travel

BCD Travel is a privately held global travel management company owned by the BCD Group. Founded in 2006, BCD Travel helps individuals travel smart and advises travel and procurement managers on how to grow their travel programs. Headquartered in Utrecht, the Netherlands, with U.S. headquarters in Atlanta, Georgia, BCD Travel serves clients across the globe, maintaining operations in over 110 countries across six continents. In the past, BCD Travel has hired for temporary, occasional, alternative schedule, and remote jobs in

travel and hospitality. The company employs over 12,000 professionals and offers flexible schedules and many opportunities for training
and career development. BCD Travel's services include managed
travel, which helps travelers, managers, and executives travel smarter,
and business travel consulting.

Past Flexible Jobs at BCD Travel
Corporate Travel Consultant

Corporate travel consultant needed for a full-time opportunity. This
is a remote position with flexible hours. Will provide travel consulta-
tions and assist customers. Three years' travel industry experience
required. Bachelor's degree preferred.

Global Program Manager

Candidate with 5 years corporate travel industry experience needed
to handle client retention, travel and supplier contract negotiation,
business consolidation, sales, financials, and business planning for
client travel programs. Partial remote job with travel.

Belay

Website: belaysolutions.com
Headquarters: Atlanta, Georgia
Industry: Administrative
Remote jobs: virtual assistant, bookkeeper

About Belay

Belay is a virtual solutions company with an entirely remote team,
offering web support, copywriting, and bookkeeping. Flexible jobs
posted in the past include remote, full-time, and part-time jobs in
administrative, consulting, sales, accounting and finance, and HR
and recruiting fields. Some contractors work as little as 10 hours per
week (the minimum) while others choose to work 40-plus hours per
week. Contractors are asked to be available to their clients Monday
through Friday, normal business hours. The firm provides ongoing
resources and support for contractors via webinars, mentors, and
coaching, and have a community where contractors can share best
practices with each other. Most contractors have at least some college, with over 75 percent having at least a bachelor's degree.
Interviews for positions are conducted over email and video- confer-

ence calls. The application process consists of two interviews along with a skills assessment. Belay provides clients with virtual administrative assistants, webmasters, and bookkeepers, and is a recognized national leader in nonprofit and church bookkeeping solutions.

Past Flexible Jobs at Belay
Bookkeeper
Needs a bachelor's degree and five years' accounting/bookkeeping experience. Pay client's bills on a weekly basis, reconcile bank statements, manage budget, perform data entry, provide clients with weekly and monthly reports.

Executive Assistant
Remote, full-time, contract job. Needs experience working with manager and a bachelor's degree. Deliver excellent customer care, can manage confidential information, maintain the executive's calendar, plan and schedule meetings, and set appointments.

BroadPath Healthcare Solutions

Website: broad-path.com
Headquarters: Tucson, Arizona
Industry: Healthcare
Remote jobs: director of service operations, provider service representative, insurance claims processor, data specialist

About BroadPath Healthcare Solutions
BroadPath Healthcare Solutions is a privately held healthcare services firm that helps providers and payers in government and commercial sectors manage the healthcare landscape. BroadPath Healthcare Solutions offers services in the categories of business, technology, and compliance, including sales and marketing, customer care, claims, administration, Medicare contracting, consulting, quality programs, compliance audits, ICD-10 services, and EHR services, among others.

As an employer, BroadPath Healthcare Solutions has supported work flexibility by posting temporary, seasonal, and remote jobs in medical and health, insurance, and customer service. Prior vacancies also include bilingual and analyst jobs, as well as positions that feature flexible and alternative schedules. In addition to providing a flexible work environment with ongoing opportunities for advancement, staffers are offered competitive compensation and other perks.

Today, BroadPath's client list includes many of the most successful healthcare organizations in the country, such as UnitedHealth, Centene, Tufts, Anthem, and several Blue Cross Blue Shield plans, including Alabama, Arkansas, Kansas City, North Carolina, and North Dakota.

Past Flexible Jobs at BroadPath Healthcare Solutions
Credentialing Specialist

The work-at-home provider credentialing specialist will be responding to inquiries, processing and tracking credentialing applications, and maintaining the credentialing database. Must have at least two years' health insurance experience.

Health Insurance Claims Processor

Work from home position. Responsibilities include processing claims for inbound health insurance, schedule adherence, and demonstrate strong active listening skills and a strong eye for detail. One year of relevant work experience is needed.

Cactus Communications

Website: cactusglobal.com
Headquarters: Mumbai, Maharashtra, India
Industry: Communications
Remote jobs: editor, medical writer, academic research evaluation

About Cactus Communications

Cactus Communications, founded in 2002, is a privately held company and a provider of communication solutions specializing in academia and pharmaceutical and device companies. Working with academic societies, researchers, universities, and publishers, the company offers training, education, and transcription services. In addition, Cactus Communications offers English-language workshops, publication support services, medical communications, scientific and academic editing, and translation services.

In the past, the company has hired for full-time and part-time, freelance and remote jobs in communications, editing, writing, translation, and transcription, including work-from-anywhere jobs. Headquartered in Mumbai, Maharashtra, India, Cactus Communications has five offices worldwide, in Pennsylvania, Japan, China, Singapore, and South Korea. It comprises nearly 500 staff members and 1,000 freelance contractors located across the globe.

Past Flexible Jobs at Cactus Communications
Editor, Materials Science
Seeking a freelance editor familiar with materials science to revise academic manuscripts. Candidate must have a college degree/expertise and prior editing experience.

Editor, Business and Finance
A contract opportunity is available for a candidate in business and finance. Must have an advanced degree or expertise in subject area, and have strong grammatical skills. This remote position has a flexible schedule.

Concentrix

Website: concentrix.com
Headquarters: Fremont, California
Industry: Business services
Remote jobs: sales and service representative

About Concentrix
Founded in 1983, Concentrix is a global provider of business services that enable high-quality communication between clients and customers. It delivers client services in more than 70 languages from locations in over 40 countries. It offers remote work, full-time and part-time, seasonal, temporary, and a.m. and p.m. shifts. The company has operated a far-reaching work-from-home program since 2004, allowing agents to work from the comfort of their home offices around the world. Moreover, staffers can take their work with them when they move if they choose to relocate for any reason. The firm describes its work-from-home candidates as "effective communicators who provide great customer service and are disciplined, flexible, focused, independent, organized, and personable." Clients range across the financial, automotive, energy, tourism, technology, ecommerce, insurance, healthcare, media,

retail, public sector, and transportation industries. Concentrix specializes in providing clients with marketing, analytics, consulting, financial, technology, and customer lifecycle management solutions.

Past Flexible Jobs at Concentrix
Senior Manager Talent Acquisition
He or she is responsible for the development and execution of an effective short-term recruiting strategy. Bachelor's degree and prior related experience required.

Sales and Service Representative
Interface with customers via outbound and inbound calls, offer customer service support and the resolution of problems with billing, service cancellations, and order status. At least one year of experience is needed. Work partially at home position; or full-time, 100 percent remote job.

CVS Health

Website: cvshealth.com
Headquarters: Woonsocket, Rhode Island
Industry: Medical and health
Remote jobs: nurse, pharmacist, recruiter

About CVS Health
CVS Health, a leading healthcare company, has hired for remote, part-time, flexible schedule, and occasional jobs in numerous disciplines in and beyond medical and health, such as account management, sales, insurance, and customer service jobs. As an employer, CVS Health offers eligible associates a comprehensive benefits package that includes medical coverage, paid time off, educational assistance programs, and more.

Past Flexible Jobs at CVS Health
Strategic Pricing Director
Strategic Pricing Director is needed for a remote opportunity. Candidate will develop pricing strategies to optimize gross margin within existing contract parameters. Bachelor's degree and prior related experience required.

Registered Nurse
Candidate will use clinical expertise to conduct telephonic health assessments and provide appropriate education to members in multiple disease populations. Five years' recent clinical experience and RN license required. Optional remote job after 3–6 months training.

Dell

Website: dell.com
Headquarters: Round Rock, Texas
Industry: Computer technology
Remote jobs: program manager, account executive, consultant, sales executive

About Dell
Dell Technologies is a multinational technology company based in Round Rock, Texas, with offices throughout the world. Today, the brand is part of a family of businesses that also includes Dell EMC, Pivotal, RSA, Secureworks, Virtustream, and VMware.

Seeking applicants who want to play a role in the digital future, Dell Technologies offers multiple opportunities for flexible work through its Connected Workplace (jobs.dell.com/work-flexibility) program. The company provides team members with the freedom to choose the "work style that best fulfills their needs on the job and in their personal lives." Flexible work arrangements provided by Dell Technologies include flexible schedules, remote work, job sharing, part-time schedules, and compressed workweeks. Products, services, and solutions offered by Dell Technologies and its family of brands are wide in range, from cloud-based products to data protection, networking, servers, and more. Across these areas, the company offers industry, infrastructure, embedded and edge, OEM, and workforce solutions, as well as consulting, education, cloud, deployment, residency, managed, and support services.

Past Flexible Jobs at Dell
Account Executive
Focus on farming and hunting sales opportunities to pass through large accounts and promote EMC converged platform solutions,

ensure value proposition to meet customer requirements, and perform account/industry analysis.

Project Manager—Cyber Security

Project manager needed for a remote option position requiring a relevant BA/BS, eight-plus years' experience in project management, and past cybersecurity-focused experience. CISSP or related professional certification a plus. Will oversee project tasks.

EF Education First

Website: ef.edu
Headquarters: Cambridge, Massachusetts
Industry: Education
Remote jobs: language teacher, copywriter, content writer, college counselor, IT coordinator

About EF Education First

EF Education First is an international language training and educational travel company that offers academic degrees and cultural exchange services. The company's associates are entrepreneurial, innovative, and culturally diverse, and eligible staffers receive generous benefits, such as healthcare, a 401(k) with 25 percent company match, paid time off, and the opportunity to travel.

In the past, EF has offered part-time, flexible schedule, freelance, and up to 100 percent remote jobs for applicants across the United States, as well as remote jobs featuring the option to work from anywhere in the world. In addition to education and training jobs, the company has posted opportunities in computer and IT, writing, human services, and nonprofit and philanthropy fields, among others.

EF Education First was founded in 1965 and now employs 37,000 people. The variety of Education First programs include online and location-based language schools for businesses and individuals, high school and university education, educational tours for Canadian and American students and adults, and cultural exchange programs.

Past flexible jobs at EF Education First
French Curriculum and Content Writer

Seeking a French curriculum writer for a work-from-home position. Create/edit academic content, develop components for audiences, and collaborate with team members. Must have a bachelor's degree and be fluent in French.

Online ESL Teacher for Kids
Seeking an ESL teacher for a work-from-home opportunity. Will teach online courses to children in China ages 5–10. Must have a bachelor's degree and be a native English speaker. Contract position, $13–$16 per hour.

Hibu

Website: hibu.com
Headquarters: Reading, England, United Kingdom
Industry: Sales
Remote jobs: account executive

About Hibu
Hibu provides a full range of digital marketing solutions for local businesses across the United Kingdom, Spain, and the United States. The company maintains global corporate headquarters in Reading, United Kingdom, and U.S. locations in King of Prussia, Pennsylvania; Cedar Rapids, Iowa; and East Meadow, New York. Flexible Hibu jobs posted in the past include alternative schedule, temporary, part-time, and full-time, remote jobs with flexible schedules in marketing, account management, sales, advertising and PR, and business development. Hibu provides paid training, referral bonuses, education assistance, retirement plans, and health benefits where eligible. The team at Hibu works with business clients to deliver digital marketing campaigns. Its products and services include website development and management, online directory listings, search engine optimization, and social campaign creation and management.

Past Flexible Jobs at Hibu
Digital Account Executive
Digital account executive needed for a full-time opportunity. This position is partially remote with frequent travel involved. Will develop marketing programs. One year of relevant experience required. Google and Facebook certifications preferred.

Account Executive, Outside Sales

Seeking account executive for full-time, remote role with some travel. Work with business owners to create marketing solutions. Must have 2-plus years of sales, marketing, and/or advertising experience, and a valid driver's license. Bachelor's degree a plus.

Hilton

Website: Hilton.com
Headquarters: McLean, Virginia
Industry: Travel/hospitality
Remote jobs: sales, special events manager, customer service

About Hilton

A global hotel management company in business since 1919, Hilton's network encompasses 5,800 properties spanning 114 countries and territories. A supporter of work flexibility, Hilton has posted part-time, flexible schedule, freelance, temporary, and remote jobs in diverse professional fields in and beyond travel and hospitality in the past. According to its website, the company offers stable, year-round work with benefits, training, and career growth opportunities, believing "the more flexible we make the work environment, the more we can provide our team members with what they need to manage their lives while feeling trusted and valued."

Past Flexible Jobs at Hilton
Head of Catering and Events, Americas

Head of catering and events needed for a full-time opportunity. This is a remote position with frequent travel involved. Will ensure that revenue goals are met. Five years' related experience and bachelor's degree or ten years' experience required.

Events Technology Manager

Seeking an Events Technology Manager for a full-time remote role. He or she will partner with business owners and the team's special events managers, who will be executing and planning the events. Prior relevant experience is required. Travel.

Humana

Website: humana.com
Headquarters: Louisville, Kentucky
Industry: Healthcare
Remote jobs: sales manager, medical director, business and technology lead, sales executive

About Humana

Based in Louisville, Kentucky, Humana is a leading healthcare company that offers an array of health, wellness, and insurance products and services. Founded in 1961, Humana now represents over 13.8 million medical members nationwide and is recognized as the nation's third-largest health insurance provider. Humana employs a team of approximately 49,000 associates, and as an employer offers a competitive salary and benefits program to eligible team members, including generous paid time off, tuition assistance, and career mentoring. Flexible Humana jobs offered in the past have included full-time, remote jobs and part-time jobs in a number of career fields, such as human services, medical and health, sales, insurance, and consulting.

Past Flexible Jobs at Humana
Lead, Cyber Data Protection Management

Will guide architects on embedding techniques, drive products from design completion to volume production release, support product evaluation, and analyze/provide technical support. Bachelor's degree required; master's preferred. Full-time, 100 percent remote.

Medical Director

Oversee service of healthcare professionals to ensure compliance, quality, and appropriateness. Review claims, provide direction, and conduct analysis. Work-at-home role requires an MD or DO, board certification, medical license, and five years' experience.

JPMorgan Chase

Website: jpmorganchase.com
Headquarters: New York, New York
Industry: Accounting and finance
Remote jobs: client services, onboarding associate

About JPMorgan Chase

JPMorgan Chase is a global financial services firm and the sixth-largest bank in the world by assets, which exceed $2.5 trillion. As an employer, JPMorgan Chase offers a range of job opportunities, from internships and new graduate programs to reentry programs for military personnel and veterans. In the past, JPMorgan Chase has posted flexible jobs in accounting and finance, marketing, operations, computer and IT, sales, and more. These opportunities have featured work-life balance with temporary, part-time, and remote jobs. As eligible, associates have also enjoyed a range of benefits and perks, from healthcare to wellness programs to discounts on travel, entertainment, and more.

Past Flexible Jobs at JPMorgan Chase
Client Processing Specialist

Full-time position. Will reconcile activity, interpret legal agreements, monitor fees, and provide information. Bachelor's degree and 2-plus years' related experience required. Flexible schedule. Remote option.

Retirement Business Director

Telecommute position managing assets, retirement business, and providing advisement. Must have 5 or more years of financial services experience and solid sales skills. FINRA Series 7 and 63 licenses are required.

K12 Jobs

Website: k12.com
Headquarters: Herndon, Virginia
Industry: Education and training
Remote jobs: online teacher, counselor, special education

About K12

K12 is a provider of online educational programs and solutions for youth in kindergarten through twelfth grade. In addition to workplace flexibility, eligible team members receive benefits, such as paid time off and medical coverage. In the past, K12 has offered temporary, freelance, flexible schedule, and remote jobs in education and training, including full-time jobs that can be done from any U.S.

region. K12 offers web-based interactive classes and learning modules. Its mission is to provide high-quality, personalized education experiences online to serve students "in the home or on the road." Educational solutions offered by K12 are designed to benefit military families, homeschooled children, advanced learners, career-minded students, athletes, and traveling performers. The company operates online private schools that include the Keystone School, the George Washington University Online High School, and K12 International Academy.

Past Flexible Jobs at K12
English Teacher
Deliver instruction, support, and guidance to 6–8 general ed students in an online classroom. Must have a bachelor's degree, six months of teaching experience, and certification. New teachers welcome. Remote, full-time job with little travel.

Career Counselor
Career counselor is needed for a full-time remote position. He or she will promote student success by providing preventative services and responding to identified needs. Must have strong communication skills. Bachelor's degree and prior related experience required.

Kaplan

Website: kaplan.com
Headquarters: Fort Lauderdale, Florida
Industry: Education and training
Remote jobs: instructor, program manager

About Kaplan
Kaplan is a for-profit educational institution that now operates in over 30 countries worldwide. The company employs over 19,000 individuals, many of whom benefit from flexible work arrangements like part-time and remote jobs in education and training and other fields. Supplementing its flexible work option, Kaplan delivers academic instruction and support, specializing in four areas: K–12 programs, online higher education, professional training, and test preparation.

Past Flexible Jobs at Kaplan
In-Person Teacher Manager
Virtual job for candidate who will manage teachers for HR, payroll, performance, quality and development needs, identify recruiting needs and serve as hiring manager for in-person teachers. Bachelor's degree required. Management experience preferred.

LSAT Prep Instructor
Seeking LSAT prep instructor for remote position, teaching mainly on weekday evenings and weekends. Must have LSAT score in the 90th percentile or be willing to retest, authorization to work in the United States, and be 18 years of age or older.

Kelly Services

Website: Kellyservices.com
Headquarters: Troy, Michigan
Industry: Staffing
Remote jobs: data entry operator, administrative assistant, software tester, data analyst

About Kelly Services
Since 1946, Kelly Services has connected skilled workers with top businesses and Fortune 100 companies in a broad range of industries. The company offers a comprehensive range of flexible work arrangements, including direct-hire, freelance, part-time, temporary-to-hire, and remote, work-from-home opportunities. These have been posted in various career divisions for experienced applicants with relevant skills and college degrees, depending on the role.

Kelly Services specializes in placing workers in diverse industries, such as accounting and finance, administrative, automotive, engineering, information technology, life sciences, call centers, and much more. With thousands of client relationships worldwide, Kelly Services annually provides nearly half a million workers with employment opportunities.

Past flexible jobs at Kelly Services
Recruiter
Work with managers to identify staffing needs. Manage job listings and candidate outreach to fill roles. Requires a bachelor's degree

and full-cycle recruiting experience. Temporary 6-month contract with full-time hours and remote options; $30–$35/hour. Full-time, option for remote job.

Medical Proofreader
Needs bachelor's degree and experience proofing and labeling documents. Pays $35.00 an hour. Proof printed packaging and labeling files, correct errors in accordance with internal brand style guide standards. Full-time, option for remote job.

LanguageLine Solutions

Website: languageline.com
Headquarters: Monterey, California
Industry: Translation
Remote jobs: interpreter, software engineer

About LanguageLine Solutions
LanguageLine Solutions was launched in 1982 to provide a more effective communication method for non-English speakers. Today, the company is a leading provider of face-to-face, over-the-phone, and videoconference interpreting and document translation services for clients in healthcare, government, and business sectors worldwide. LanguageLine Solutions maintains a large remote workforce of phone and video interpreters, as well as on-site interpreters and corporate employees. Based in Monterey, California, the company has offices throughout the United States, the UK, Mexico, Canada, Puerto Rico, the Dominican Republic, and Costa Rica.

In the past, LanguageLine Solutions has hired for part-time, alternative schedule, freelance, and remote jobs in bilingual, translation, computer and IT, customer service, and additional fields, including U.S. National jobs for applicants nationwide. To qualify, according to its website, passionate individuals should ideally possess a range of role-related skills and qualifications. Examples include strong listening, retention, and note-taking abilities and experience in language-related fields.

Past Flexible Jobs at LanguageLine Solutions
Strategic Account Executive
Sell language solutions to enterprise and healthcare organizations within a defined base of prospective and current customers. Must have a bachelor's degree and language services industry experience. Remote with 50 percent travel.

Spanish Interpreter
Handle calls on-demand and render the meaning of conversations between Spanish and English speakers. Must have a high school diploma and be English/Spanish fluent. Some experience preferred. Full-time, remote position.

Lionbridge

Website: Lionbridge.com
Headquarters: Waltham, Massachusetts
Industry: Software and business (language translation)
Remote jobs: creative designer, social media assessor, project manager, scheduling assistant

About Lionbridge
Founded in 1996, Lionbridge is a leader in language translation services and also offers content and testing, global marketing, machine intelligence, multilingual websites, and engineering services. The company is headquartered in Waltham, Massachusetts, with operations throughout the United States and internationally. Team members work from home or from one of the company's 47 offices spanning 26 countries. Lionbridge has offered part-time, freelance, and remote jobs through the Smart Crowd global community database (thesmartcrowd.lionbridge.com), a program designed to provide work-at-home opportunities. Past postings include positions in diverse fields, such as editing, research, internet and ecommerce, translation, and bilingual jobs.

Past flexible jobs at Lionbridge
Quality Controller
Remote role for candidate who will manage the performance of cloud-based resources and conduct root cause analysis of performance issues, create eLearning materials, and host webinars. SQL

experience and experience designing eLearning content preferred. Full-time, 100 percent remote job, U.S. National.

Project Manager
Will create project plans, work with team, drive project timelines, manage schedule, develop solutions and budget forecasts. Bachelor's degree and 3-plus years' related experience required. Full-time, 100 percent remote job, U.S. National.

Liveops

Website: Liveops.com
Headquarters: Scottsdale, Arizona
Industry: Customer service
Remote jobs: customer service representative, licensed insurance agent, health care resource specialist

About Liveops
Hundreds of companies around the world turn to Liveops for its cloud contact center and customer service solutions. Headquartered in Scottsdale, Arizona, the company maintains additional offices in Dayton, Ohio; Portland, Oregon; and Redwood City, California. The company frequently offers work-from-home jobs in the areas of customer service, medical and health, insurance, and sales, to name a few, for entry-level and experienced professionals with role-related skills and qualifications. In the past, Liveops has hired for both full-time and part-time, remote jobs throughout the United States.

Launched in 2001, Liveops is one of the largest marketplaces for call center workers. The team connects more than 20,000 independent call center agents with businesses around the world in a wide range of industries, including the financial, high-tech, retail, healthcare, and insurance sectors. Liveops was awarded the prestigious Alfred P. Sloan Award for Business Excellence in Workplace Flexibility.

Past flexible jobs at Liveops
Customer Service Representative
Handles inbound and outbound calls, helps customers understand insurance options, and assists them with insurance applications. Requires life and health insurance producer licensure.

Pays $.30/min of talk time plus commission. Remote-based, contract position, 100 percent remote job, U.S. National.

Licensed Insurance Agent

An insurance agent is needed to take inbound calls from customers, follow up with warm leads, and assist customers in finding policies. Must have an active life/health insurance license. Contract, work-from-home position, 100 percent remote job, U.S. National.

Motion Recruitment Partners

Website: motionrecruitment.com
Headquarters: Boston, Massachusetts
Industry: Recruiting
Remote jobs: recruiting, payroll manager, benefits coordinator

About Modern Recruitment Partners

Motion Recruitment Partners, founded in 1989, is the parent company of three industry-leading recruitment agencies: Jobspring Partners, Sevenstep, and Workbridge. Headquartered in Boston, Massachusetts, Motion Recruitment Partners has hired for temporary, freelance, and remote jobs in computer and IT, software development, writing, editing, graphic design, and other creative and technical fields in the past. The company also offers a comprehensive benefits package to eligible team members, including medical coverage, 401(k) plans, and pretax commuter benefits.

In particular, Jobspring Partners and Workbridge Associates are two leading providers of IT contractor staffing, direct-hire, and permanent placement in more than 10 North American markets. Through a network of 400 recruiters across 21 offices, both companies specialize in network security, Microsoft development, open-source development, UI/UX design and development, and mobile development.

Past Flexible Jobs at Motion Recruitment Partners
Software Developer

Software developer needed for a freelance, remote option position paying $50/hour. Three-plus years' experience with quality assurance automation, familiarity with writing automation scripts and conducting tests required.

Data Engineer
Full-time position. Will build ETL pipelines, perform hands-on coding and provide expertise. Bachelor's degree and 3-plus years' related experience required. Flexible schedule, $140,000/year.

Parallon

Website: parallon.com
Headquarters: Nashville, Tenn.
Industry: Medical and health
Remote jobs: scheduler, patient account representative, appeals specialist

About Parallon
Headquartered in Nashville, Tennessee, with operational locations across the country, Parallon was founded as part of HCA Healthcare in 2011 to provide revenue cycle management services for hospitals and healthcare organizations. As an employer, it has offered business, operational, and clinical career tracks in fields like medical and health, administrative, customer service, accounting and finance, insurance, and more. Parallon provides full-service consulting and advising services, revenue-cycle services, group-purchasing support, supply chain services, healthcare information technology, and workforce management solutions.

Past Flexible Jobs at Parallon
Overpayment Analyst
Remote, work-at-home position analyzing overpayments, performing research, and resolving issues. Monitor accounts, resolve balances, and initiate refunds. Must have a HS diploma and one year of relevant experience.

Medicaid Eligibility Advocate
Conduct screenings/assessment of patient financial requirements, screen/evaluate patients for existing insurance coverage, and maintain follow-up with patient and government agency caseworkers. HS diploma required. Full-time, 100 percent remote.

Pearson

Website: pearson.com/us/
Headquarters: London, England
Industry: Education and training
Remote jobs: content specialist, test administrator, customer service

About Pearson

Pearson is an international learning company offering an extensive range of content, tools, products, and services for educators and learners of all ages. Headquartered in London, United Kingdom, Pearson maintains a team of 32,000 individuals across 70 countries. Pearson offers flexible jobs in many professional fields in and beyond education and training and has posted temporary, freelance, seasonal, occasional, part-time, flexible schedule, and work-from-home jobs in the past. The firm looks for applicants who demonstrate role-related experience and training to apply for open positions. Other valued qualifications include the ability to communicate effectively and utilize technology. Examples of standard benefits include health coverage, paid time off, and retirement savings plans, among others.

Pearson's products and services include content and technology platforms, such as MyLab, SuccessMaker, and enVisionMATH; assessments like A levels, GCSEs, and TestNav school assessments; and services like Pearson VUE and the Pearson Institute of Higher Education. Pearson now serves millions of students and teachers across the globe every day.

Past Flexible Jobs at Pearson
E-Director Digital Sales

Recruit, develop, and hire talent, distribute and oversee travel and expense budget allocations, and oversee partnerships with localized sales teams. At least five years of sales performance experience is needed. Work-from-home position with travel required.

Training Consultant

Deliver on-site and virtual training to an academy staff, assist teachers with monitoring student performance, and assist teachers with advancing practices as online educators. Work remotely from home; must be able to travel. Requires three years of experience. Full-time, partial remote job, U.S. National.

Philips

Website: usa.philips.com
Headquarters: Amsterdam, North Holland, Netherlands
Industry: Medical and health; computer/IT
Remote jobs: help desk technician, project manager, financial analyst

About Philips
A diversified company founded in 1891 and one of the world's largest electronics companies, Philips is a provider of acute care, home healthcare, oral healthcare, lighting applications, contemporary art, watches and jewelry, photographs, and energy-efficient lighting solutions for global markets.

Philips employs over 100,000 professionals across 100 countries around the world and offers a range of employment opportunities in sales, marketing, medical and health, account management, and computer and IT, among other areas. In the past, Philips has posted full-time and part-time, partial to 100 percent remote jobs.

Past Flexible Jobs at Philips
Radiologist Support Assistant
Support assistant needed for a remote, third shift–position updating system records, maintaining communications, identifying and documenting issues, conducting follow-ups, answering inquiries, and monitoring queues. Medical terminology knowledge required.

Medical Transcriptionist
Seeking a medical transcriptionist for a full-time remote role. He or she will draft and transcribe radiology report. Must have strong computer skills. At least one year of relevant experience is required. Multiple shifts available.

PRA Health Sciences

Website: prahs.com
Headquarters: Raleigh, North Carolina
Industry: Medical and health, computer/IT
Remote jobs: program analyst, research associate, medical copy editor

About PRA Health Sciences

PRA Health Sciences is an award-winning, global contract research firm that focuses on assisting companies to develop life-improving and lifesaving drugs, as well as diagnostic tools, in the fields of neurology, psychiatry, oncology, hematology, infectious diseases, cardiometabolic diseases, immunology, respiratory conditions, gastroenterology, and genitourinary diseases. Headquartered in Raleigh, North Carolina, PRA Health Sciences manages offices in over 80 countries and employs more than 12,000 associates.

For flexible positions at PRA Health Sciences, leadership has preferred applicants who are highly "motivated and passionate about shaping the future of clinical development" to join its team. In the past, PRA Health Sciences has posted a wide range of remote, part-time, and temporary jobs in science, medical and health, research, operations, and computer and IT fields.

Past Flexible Jobs at PRA Health Sciences
Senior Contracts and Grants Analyst

Senior analyst needed for a remote job requiring a BA/BS, one-plus year contract-focused experience, English fluency, clinical contract knowledge, and excellent negotiating skills. JD degree a plus. Will perform negotiations, resolve issues, analyze data.

Study Manager

Provide assistance to the study team and SM study lead with operational clinical study, conduct, lead a study, and track study timelines. At least two years of experience in clinical research is needed. Work-from- home position.

Robert Half International

Website: roberthalf.com
Headquarters: Menlo Park, CA
Industry: HR and recruiting
Remote jobs: recruiting, payroll manager, benefits coordinator

About Robert Half

Founded in 1948, Robert Half International is a global professional staffing and consulting firm. Robert Half offers eligible team members a comprehensive benefits package that includes paid time off, medical coverage, and the opportunity to participate in its corporate citizenship program, which enables them to contribute to local and global charities. With career opportunities in wide-ranging fields, such as HR and recruiting, accounting and finance, computer and IT, administrative, and legal, Robert Half International has hired for part-time, freelance, temporary, and remote jobs in the past.

Past Flexible Jobs at Robert Half International
Human Resources—HR—Generalist

Will provide operational support, conduct onboarding, lead initiatives, resolve issues and advise managers. Bachelor's degree and 10-plus years' related experience required. Travel.

Accountant

Close out the 2019 books and help review the work of the bookkeeper and provide them with support. Must have a bachelor's degree and recent relevant financial experience. Temporary, part-time role with flexible hours.

Salesforce

Website: salesforce.com
Headquarters: San Francisco, California
Industry: Computer and IT
Remote jobs: graphic designer, software engineer, operations analyst

About Salesforce

Salesforce helps businesses of all sizes and from all industries connect with their customers. Past and present customers include BarkBox, Carlo's Bakery, Gilt, Spotify, Square, Coca-Cola Enterprises, GE, Kimberly-Clark, and Philips. In the past, Salesforce has offered flexible jobs in fields like sales, account management, consulting, software development, and business development.

Past Flexible Jobs at Salesforce
Senior Graphic Designer

The senior graphic designer will be developing visual designs, helping produce marketing materials, and leading creative projects. Requires advanced Adobe Creative Suite skills and seven years' agency experience. Work-from-home position.

Senior Account Executive, Platform, Cloud Sales

The senior account executive will establish a platform sales strategy, develop new customers, create sales plans, act as a trusted advisor, and negotiate and close deals. Must have at least five years' solution sales experience. Remote-based opportunity.

SAP

Website: sap.com
Headquarters: Walldorf, Baden-Wurttemberg, Germany
Industry: Computer and IT
Remote jobs: project manager, compliance specialist, technical writer

About SAP

SAP, founded in 1972, provides clients in over 180 countries with software and data-processing solution services while utilizing the skills and knowledge of the company's more than 65,000 employees. Furthermore, SAP offers small and midsize enterprises digital transformation and machine-learning services. As an employer, SAP offers a flexible, diverse company culture with over 15 percent of employees working from home. The company regularly hires for freelance, temporary, and remote jobs and has previously posted opportunities in fields such as computer and IT, software development, HR and recruiting, sales, and accounting and finance. Its solutions include analytics, application platform and infrastructure, data management, IT management, and security software. Headquartered in Walldorf, Baden-Württemberg, Germany, SAP maintains U.S. headquarters in Newton Square, Pennsylvania.

Past Flexible Jobs at SAP
International Organic Social Media Marketing Senior Specialist
The social media manager will create and implement the content strategy, define the process for content publishing, manage reporting, and syndicate and localize content. At least three to five years' experience required.

Solution Advisor Expert
Full-time remote position will work with teams to generate pricing, provide ongoing deal support to sales teams, conduct detailed technical workshops with customers. Must have a bachelor's degree and five years of experience. Some travel.

Sutherland

Website: sutherlandglobal.com
Headquarters: Pittsford, New York
Industry: Customer Service
Remote jobs: tech support, customer service, underwriter

About Sutherland
Founded in 1986 and headquartered in Pittsford, New York, a suburb of Rochester, Sutherland is a worldwide process transformation company. As an employer, Sutherland seeks driven candidates passionate about excellence who embrace technology and demonstrate independence, exceptional communication skills, and can "thrive without face-to-face interaction," according to the Remote.co site.

In the past, Sutherland jobs have featured "fully remote/work-from-home and part-time positions," as well as "hub- and- spoke positions" in which employees come into a physical location for a period of time and then transition to work from their home office with occasional on-site meetings or training courses. With more than 60 global operation centers, over 120 clients, and 38,000 employees in 19 countries, and combining data analytics and design thinking, the company helps clients in multiple industries. Sutherland provides customer-facing services, back-office solutions, and technology-enabled services.

Past Flexible Jobs at Sutherland
Underwriter
Seeking candidate with three to five years' mortgage underwriting experience to be responsible for approval/decline decisions on incoming applications consistent with client policies and based on employment profile and credit strength. Virtual position.

Life and Health Licensed Sales
A work-at-home life/health sales associate is needed to handle inbound calls, build relationships with customers, and improve quality results. High school diploma and one year of experience in secondary education required.

Sykes

Website: sykes.com
Headquarters: Tampa, Florida
Industry: Customer service
Remote jobs: customer support agent, executive assistant, senior director of client management

About Sykes
Sykes, founded in 1977, is a provider of customer contact management solutions to clients worldwide. It has previously offered remote jobs in more than 40 U.S. states and in countries around the world. Past opportunities include bilingual, call center, and customer service jobs, to name a few.

Depending on eligibility, the employer offers associates a comprehensive benefits package that may include medical coverage, scheduling flexibility, and professional growth opportunities, among other perks.

Sykes serves companies around the world, providing many Fortune 1000 and Global 2000 businesses across the leisure, technology, communications, transportation, financial services, and healthcare markets with sales, multichannel, technical, and analytical support. Headquartered in Tampa, Florida, Sykes has an additional corporate office in Denver, Colorado.

Past flexible positions at Sykes
Customer Service Representative
Responsible for assisting with issues and solving problems for customers in a virtual call center. Must have computer skills, an empathetic personality, and a strong phone presence. All telecommuting. Candidates need to be able to work in the city or state specified. Full-time work-from-home job opportunity.

Transcom

Website: transcom.com
Headquarters: Stockholm, Uppland, Sweden
Industry: Customer service
Remote jobs: technical support representative, payroll administrator, customer service agent

About Transcom
A global business, Transcom offers customer care, sales, technical support, and credit management services. It employs a team of nearly 30,000 people and offers eligible associates a competitive salary and benefits package. Furthermore, it enables staffers to grow careers "while working from the comfort and convenience" of their own homes, according to the website. In the past, the company has hired for freelance, part-time, and 100 percent remote jobs in call centers, customer service, computer and IT, communications, and sales fields, among others.

Headquartered in Stockholm, Uppland, Sweden, Transcom operates 55 global contact centers that offer on-site job opportunities around the world. In North America, however, team members work entirely from home. The company's remote job opportunities are available in over 30 U.S. states and six Canadian provinces. Transcom seeks "tech-savvy applicants who share its passion for people, demonstrate strong multitasking abilities, and want to build a flexible, work-from-home career."

Past Flexible Job at Transcom
Technical Support Representative
Full-time, remote job. Pays $13.00 after training. Needs to be 18-plus, have a HS diploma, and previous call center support experience is a

plus. Engage with callers, actively listen, analyze and isolate tech issues, and navigate multiple applications.

TranscribeMe!

Website: transcribeme.com
Headquarters: San Francisco, California
Industry: Information technology, translation
Remote jobs: transcriptionist

About TranscribeMe!

Founded in 2011, TranscribeMe! is an information technology and services company specializing in worldwide translation services. An advocate for flexible work arrangements, TranscribeMe! offers "100% remote positions" and seeks "workers who are willing to learn and grow" with the company. Operating as "a 24/7 company," it values "workers in all time zones" available "all hours of the day" and employs individuals internationally. In the past, TranscribeMe! has posted completely remote jobs, and work-from-anywhere jobs with full-time, part-time, alternative, and flexible schedules in data entry, transcription, translation, editing, and bilingual fields. A global company headquartered in San Francisco, California, TranscribeMe has an office in New Zealand and a division in Japan.

Past Flexible Jobs at TranscribeMe!
Transcriptionist

Seeking remote full-time transcriptionist to transcribe audio and video into quality text. Will be able to choose your own hours. Having a reliable internet connection and computer is required. Must have a high school diploma.

Copywriter

Seeking a copywriter for a part-time remote opportunity to compose SEO-friendly content. Candidate will best determine the content to prioritize. Must have strong writing skills. Prior related experience required. Contract project-based role.

TTEC

Website: ttec.com
Headquarters: Englewood, Colorado
Industry: Business operations
Remote jobs: Salesforce developer, software engineer, consultant, web developer

About TTEC

TTEC, launched in 1982, is a business process outsourcing company for clients in broad industries, from financial services and logistics to travel and entertainment. The firm has hired for both full-time and part-time, remote jobs in customer service, computer and IT, consulting, marketing, and sales fields, to name a few. TTEC comprises over 50,000 professionals who work across six continents, including nearly 20,000 home-based associates worldwide.

Past Flexible Jobs at TTEC
Principal, Sales Engineering

Full-time. Responsibilities include helping develop leads, building partner relationships in support of business development efforts, conducting solution design meetings, and developing design details. Travel required.

Full-stack Developer

Full-time. Work directly with the team and lead developer to identify design needs of application features and assist with troubleshooting and verifying bugs. Knowledge of test-driven development, HTML/CSS, and JavaScript is needed.

UnitedHealth Group

Website: unitedhealthgroup.com
Headquarters: Minneapolis, Minnesota
Industry: Healthcare

Remote jobs: product director, medical director, health and wellness coach, call center nurseAbout UnitedHealth Group
UnitedHealth Group is a diversified healthcare company comprised of two businesses: United Healthcare, a provider of benefits and insurance coverage; and Optum, a leading provider of technology and information-enabled health services. As an employer, UnitedHealth Group offers a comprehensive benefits package to eligible employees and has offered part-time, temporary, flexible schedule, and remote jobs in medical and health in the past. The company invests nearly $3 billion each year in technology and innovation, annually processing more than 600 billion digital transactions.

Past Flexible Jobs at UnitedHealth Group
Senior Data Engineer
Seeking a senior data engineer for a full-time, remote position requiring a college degree, five-plus years' experience with database development, one-plus year healthcare industry experience. Will generate strategy plans, identify and resolve issues.

Fertility Utilization Review RN
Utilization review nurse needed for a full-time, remote job requiring an RN license, three-plus years' fertility-focused experience in nursing, strong computer skills, and MS Office knowledge. Will perform utilization review and management, and verify services.

VIPKid

Website: Vipkid.com
Headquarters: Beijing, China
Industry: Education
Remote jobs: online English as a second language teacher

About VIPKid
VIPKid is an English language–learning services company. As an employer, VIPKid offers a competitive salary, ongoing paid training, and professional development opportunities. Based in Beijing, China, the company supports work flexibility and, in the past, has hired for part-time, freelance, and remote jobs in education and training. All of the teachers on the VIPKid platform teach from

home and decide their schedule. They can teach as many or as few hours as they prefer.

VIPKid offers ESL services to children in China and focuses on providing high-quality English education for children up to 8 years old. A team of English speakers provides one-on-one, full-immersion language and content courses based on U.S. Common Core State Standards. Students learn not only the language but about American culture and traditions. In return, American teachers learn about Chinese culture.

Past flexible jobs at VIPKid
Online ESL Teacher

Immediate need for an online ESL teacher for children. Work with students one-on-one teaching English. Courses, content, and full training provided, does require some prior teaching experience. Flexible terms, part-time contract position, up to $22/hour. Part-time, 100 percent remote job, work from anywhere.

Online Teacher

Provide one-on-one English language and content classes that are 25 minutes in length each. Bachelor's degree, at least 1 year of teaching experience, and exposure to the American/Canadian K–12 education system. Six-month contract. Part-time, 100 percent remote job, work from anywhere.

Williams-Sonoma

Website: williams-sonomainc.com
Headquarters: San Francisco, California
Industry: Retail
Remote jobs: customer service agent, technical designer, copy manager

About Williams-Sonoma

Williams-Sonoma, a specialty retailer of quality home products, was established in 1956 by Chuck Williams. It operates retail stores throughout the United States, Puerto Rico, Canada, the United Kingdom, and Australia, and is among the largest ecommerce retailers in the United States.

Via the company's Total Rewards program, eligible employees receive competitive benefits, such as a 401(k) plan, healthcare, employee discounts, quarterly sample sales, commuter benefits, and time off for volunteering. Williams-Sonoma has posted part-time, temporary, freelance, and remote jobs in the past and typically hires in the areas of art and creative, marketing, customer service, retail, and manufacturing.

Past Flexible Jobs at Williams-Sonoma
Human Resources Manager
Duties include providing HR management and generalist support, managing projects, tracking and analyzing staffing, productivity, and turnover, supporting positive employee relations, and participating in staffing initiatives.

Customer Service Agent
Responsibilities include responding to customer inquiries related to product and delivery information, recommending alternatives to out-of-stock items, processing returns, and issuing credits and replacements. $12 per hour.

Working Solutions

Website: Workingsolutions.com
Headquarters: Dallas, Texas
Industry: Customer service
Remote jobs: sales development representative, travel reservation specialist, corporate travel agent

About Working Solutions
Founded in 1996, Working Solutions is a Dallas, Texas–based provider of on-demand customer service and sales agents who work from home. In the past, Working Solutions has posted part-time, freelance, remote, and flexible schedule jobs. The company serves the energy, retail, communications, travel, financial, and healthcare industries with expertise in customer-care operations, development, technology, recruiting, security, and analytics.

The company maintains a network of more than 110,000 registered agents who work as independent contractors. Working Solutions contracts with a range of independent agents who reflect the diversity in the customers and clients it serves, including military spouses, stay-at-home parents, career-change professionals, and seniors.

Past flexible jobs at Working Solutions

Bilingual Spanish Customer Service Representative

Remote independent contractor position will provide customer service skills while guiding callers to the right solutions, research, navigate/locate answers from webpages and resources. Must be fluent in Spanish and English and have one-year experience. Part-time, 100 percent remote job, U.S. National.

Travel Reservation Specialist

Candidates need to be able to work in the city or state specified. Remote, contract job. Needs experience with complex problem resolution and 1–2 years' customer service experience. Provide excellent customer service through phone, email, or live chat support, identify and resolve problems, find customer solutions. 100 percent remote job, Cleveland, Ohio, or U.S. National.

PART
III

KERRY'S GREAT PAJAMA
JOBS WORKSHOP

Y ou made it through the nitty-gritty of the *who, what,* and *where* of remote jobs. Now it's time to get down to the basics.

I've written this workshop for those of you who are ready to take action and move to the next stage.

Before we get rolling, here's my first question: Working from home sounds like a dream job, but are you hardwired for working independently?

Some people thrive when they're surrounded by a cadre of office mates. They hate not having easy contact with a manager to encourage and lead them. For those of you who worry that could be you, the following chapters will help you do the introspection to suss that out before you step into a work environment that isn't a good fit.

For those of you who thrive on autonomy, are self-disciplined, and are energized by having a more flexible work schedule, these next chapters will get you on your way. You will fire up your job-hunting skills and discover strategies to prepare and succeed as a remote worker—both professionally and personally.

My expectation is that you will use my specific suggestions to learn new ways to job-hunt that will allow you to make smart decisions about the type of work you decide to do, where you want to do it, and how to make it "work" for you. Whether you want to work part time or a full schedule, on contract or seasonally, working remotely might just be the best work scenario you've ever had. My hope is that you'll land a position to do work you love in a setting where you can be productive, make your best effort, and, importantly, that allows you to lead a balanced life.

C H A P T E R

Avoiding Work-from-Home Scams

anger alert: I decided to kick off my workshop with some cautionary advice about the too-good-to-be-true lures for work-from-home jobs.

A jarring wake-up call for people yearning to work from home landed in late 2019. The Federal Trade Commission (FTC) ordered operators of a work-from-home scheme—Effen Ads—to pay nearly $1.5 million to settle the allegations that they used misleading, unsolicited emails to lure more than 50,000 consumers into buying work-from-home services. Here's how the Effen Ads scheme played out, according to the FTC.

If It Sounds Too Good to Be True. . .

From June 2015 through August 2017, the company and its owners, Jason Brailow and Brandon Harshbarger, e-marketed and sold a supposed work-at-home program. Consumers were told that if they paid an up-front fee (typically $97), they could make significant income with little effort working from home. All the customers needed to do was post advertising links onto websites. They were given online training videos, but, the FTC says, no advertising links to post or any other work to perform.

What's more, prospects were sent links to false online stories designed to con them into thinking the work-from-home program had received favorable reviews from news organizations like CNN and Fox News and was recommended by the likes of legendary investor Warren Buffett and personal-finance guru Suze Orman.

The director of the FTC's Bureau of Consumer Protection, Andrew Smith, said in a press release: "Consumers should be on alert for scams promising lots of income for little or no effort—if it sounds too good to be true, it probably is."

I'm a huge fan of remote work; I'm a remote worker myself, writing articles and books from my home office. I love not having to spend time and money commuting to an office, plus I enjoy the chance to take work breaks to walk my dog. But the FTC case and others like it are upsetting. It's easy to dismiss them with a "Who could be so easily duped?" shake of the head. With a growing number of Americans eager to work remotely, though, I think there's a huge need for people to understand the difference between legitimate work-from-home operations and phony ones.

One way to find a valid job where you can work from home is to search national job board sites such as Flexjobs.com, Remote.co, WAHVE (Work at Home Vintage Experts, for professionals over 50 in insurance, accounting, and human resources), Rat Race Rebellion, and Working Nomads.

Another top source: The National Telecommuting Institute (nti-athome.org/), a nonprofit that works with the Social Security Administration to fill telecommuting jobs with people who have disabilities. Founded in 1995, the telecommuting institute trains disabled people and helps them obtain the required equipment and broadband connections. The group also pairs jobseekers with mentors who help them revise their résumés, practice for interviews, and make the switch to work.

These sites screen and verify legitimate at-home opportunities.

Spotting Work-from-Home Scams

I asked Sara Sutton, CEO and founder of FlexJobs and Remote.co, for her advice on how to avoid work-from-home scams like the one described above. Here's what she told me:

"Unfortunately, scams remain a troubling component of the work-from-home job market, even as the number of legitimate remote job opportunities continues to grow," Sutton says.

"It's encouraging to see this FTC settlement, but job seekers should not let their guard down—many, many more scams still exist.

This particular scam has all the hallmarks of a typical work-from-home job scam. The scammers used recognizable, well-known media and celebrity names to lure people into assuming it was a legitimate opportunity. Those who were scammed received unsolicited emails and were asked for sensitive information and payment upfront."

Scammers are able to pull this off, she says, because "the ability to work from home would be a dream come true for many people. And because of the value people place on this way of working, scammers are able to take advantage of folks who want to find this type of job."

But she does have good news about finding work-from-home opportunities: "Real, professional remote jobs offered by legitimate companies are more common than ever. The key is knowing how to find those real jobs and how to avoid the scammers."

Sutton advises never to respond to unsolicited emails or LinkedIn messages about work-from-home opportunities, because they are almost always scams. Legitimate remote jobs are posted by companies to various job boards online, and the process for landing a remote job is very similar to a traditional job search. Anytime a potential employer is directly trying to get you to pay upfront for a "work-from-home kit," proprietary software, or any other item that is "required for the job," that is a huge red flag and you should discontinue the conversation.

Keywords like "work-from-home" and "work-at-home" are most commonly used by scammers. "Since the COVID-19 crisis, 'work from home' has been a more widely used keyword; however, we still recommend leaning on phrases such as 'remote job,' 'telecommuting job,' or 'virtual job' in your search," Sutton says. "These phrases tend to still be the ones real employers use more readily."

A simple Google search for the company's name or the job title and the word "scam" may help you determine if you've found a scam. The results may turn up news reports, Better Business Bureau complaints, court rulings, and online reviews where people warn others about that scam.

According to Sutton, these are some of the things scammers say to lure people into illegitimate offers:

- They promise jobs, money, or other big perks in exchange for very little work, or for some sort of payment or investment.
- They send unsolicited messages, emails, and other communications often with typos, grammatical errors, or misspellings. They ask for personal or sensitive information like Social Security numbers and bank accounts very quickly in the process.
- They don't give you time to think through your decision to accept the job; they often demand an answer immediately.
- Their supposed jobs often don't require experience, and anyone can start right away.

Finally, she recommends that if you've found a work-from-home job that seems fishy or not quite right, follow your instincts.

BEWARE OF SCAMS

Working at home has a nice ring to it—sometimes, too nice. Work-at-home scams have been around for decades, but in the past few years, the Federal Trade Commission has seen the number of complaints nearly double.

Two glaring red flags: jobs touted via email that promise to pay more than you ever dreamed, and firms that charge you a fee to obtain more information about a job. "Payment for the privilege of working is rarely acceptable, in our view," says Christine Durst, an internet fraud and safety expert and cofounder of RatRaceRebellion.com, a website that screens job leads on home-based jobs.

Other tips include:

- Check for complaints with the Better Business Bureau in your area and the area in which the company is headquartered. You'll also want to verify the company with your local consumer protection agency and state attorney general. For free information on work-at-home consumer issues, visit the FTC consumer information site at ftc.gov.
- Just because there aren't complaints doesn't mean the company is above board. Devious companies may settle complaints, change their names, or

move to avoid scrutiny. It's a good idea to enter the company name with the word "complaints" into a search engine to see if anything appears.

- Ask what specific tasks you'll have to perform, whether you will be paid by salary or commission, who will pay you, and when and how frequently you'll be paid.
- Never give any financial information like bank account or credit card numbers over the phone or online until you have done your research.
- Ask what the total cost to you will be, including supplies and equipment.
- Be wary of overstated claims of product effectiveness, exaggerated claims of potential earnings, and demands that you pay for something before instructions or products are provided.
- Be wary of personal testimonials that never identify the person so you can't investigate further.
- Get answers to your questions in writing.

Source: The Federal Trade Commission.

115

C H A P T E R

Work from Home Myths

Working remotely for an incredible company, clad in your stretchy yoga apparel or sweatpants, with your pooch nestled at your feet or your cat sauntering around your desktop, is appealing to many of us. The reality of a great pajama job, however, can be different than you visualize.

Here are eight myths I want to debunk straightaway:

1. **You can choose to work from anywhere in the world.** For starters, when you search for remote job openings, you will quickly discover that many work-from-home employees don't live anywhere they desire. The bulk of work-from-home positions have some geographic parameters—a country, state, or city.

    There are a few reasons for this requirement. Some companies want or need to see you in person from time to time. These in-office meetings might be to connect with clients, or take a training workshop, or launch a new initiative or project with co-workers.

    There can also be accounting, legal, licensing, and tax particulars that require a firm to hire employees who live in specific states or countries.

2. **You set your own hours.** Another common fallacy is that you can get rolling when you want and wrap up your day at your discretion. While you certainly can flip on your computer at dawn, if that's your desire, most remote employers have fixed schedules for your working hours. Of course, some employers may be open to negotiating for a flexible schedule that you adjust according to what works best for your duties (as long as you get the job done). This is important if you're a caregiver for an aging parent, or have a toddler. But that's often a case-by-case situation and may need to be reviewed intermittently.

The fact is employers who hire remote workers are hip to the out-of-sight need to trust their employees to do their work on time and put in the necessary hours. They usually put up some guard rails in terms of "office hours" to have the assurance that customers, supervisors, and teammates can easily contact the tele-working employees.

Some jobs may be a hybrid where you must be available front and center for a specific time frame (say, 9 a.m. to 12 p.m. Eastern Time) but can adjust your additional hours to suit your needs.

A set schedule can be in your best interest. My advice is that you design a daily work schedule with your boss and let your colleagues know what it is. Otherwise, you could be inviting phone calls and emails late at night and on weekends It's easy to get sucked into being free to work any time, any day. And if you love your work, like I do, you might lose track of time.

I clearly recall how difficult it was to get myself to the office in time for a 9 a.m. mandatory staff meeting every morning when I worked an office job. These days, though, I start the day by 6 a.m., seven days a week. I work many more hours than when I toiled in-house—and that's by choice. But, in truth, for the sake of my psychological well-being, I could use someone to tug me away from my laptop sometimes.

If you work for one company, try to set clear work hours to prevent phone calls, emails, and texts without boundaries on your personal time. From my experience, to work from home on a regular basis, you must be well-organized, have time management skills, and be a self-starter. If a company hires you as a remote worker, this is non-negotiable. Bear with my repetition on this point: I can't repeat this mantra enough as essential to your success as a remote worker.

3. **You won't get promoted if you work remotely.** This is increasingly becoming a myth as corporate culture is changing. Yet, to be honest, from my interviews with dozens and dozens of remote workers, I know that there is still an underlying sense in even the most remote-friendly of employers that climbing the ladder hangs on being a visible presence in an office. You can get promoted, but it will take effort on your part.

   Some employers have a hard time getting their head around the notion that you can manage others when you work from home. And managing often goes hand-in-hand with a promotion to a higher level on the corporate ladder.

   That said, when it comes to getting promoted (and the heftier pay that goes with it), you may still get tripped up in the out-of-sight, out-of-mind manager mentality—even if the promotion doesn't require managing. Your boss may just want to have more access to you. So keep this in mind and do whatever you can to be visible in other ways. The solution: regular, steady communication.

   The bad news is that if you work from home and aren't proactive about seeking promotions, your salary can flatline, which can have a nasty impact on your ability to save for retirement. When your income doesn't rise, it's tougher to ramp up the amount you put into your 401(k) or a similar employer-sponsored savings plan every year. Your employer's match will be stuck as a result, too.

   In full disclosure, you might be fine with not getting pushed up the line. I've passed on promotions to climb the editors' ranks because I knew it would be hard to be a manager while working from home. I'm not disappointed about this. That's because my meaning of career success isn't taking on more responsibility and being a boss. Plus, it wouldn't jive with my temperament.

   Your best argument for earning more pay, of course, is a great performance—wherever you do your work.

4. **You escape the office hothouse.** Another misconception of remote work is that you avoid a potentially toxic office culture, interruptions, and wasted time and can happily work away as a free agent minding your own business.

   Do that at your own peril. You probably can't avoid going into work altogether or the human connection. As I discussed above, if you want your career to progress and develop, you do need to stay connected with colleagues and managers.

To combat that, I recommend you make a conscientious effort to show up on a regular basis for meetings (some of these may be virtual for a while, but in time in-person office gatherings will return) and essential check-ins, providing, of course, you live near the employer's headquarters or a branch.

5. **Remote work is for introverts.** Au contraire. True, the best tele-commuting jobs are often ones that demand a quiet space where there are few distractions. Web-based jobs in accounting, translation, sales, public relations, medical transcription, and customer service are some of the growing areas, as we learned in Chapter 1, and there are more coming onstream all the time.

That said, you need a dollop of people-time. Loners will be sorry. You will regret it if you don't dig down and push yourself to get out of the house from time to time, and squeeze in an out-of-the-office lunch, or coffee with colleagues and bosses, providing they're in commuting distance. And the effort might take on extra meaning because in-office co-workers may have a chip on their shoulder that you have the luxury of remote working, and bad blood can develop. With a little oomph, though, you can dodge the lingering resentment that can be a potential stumbling block down the road.

At the very least, periodically pick up the phone and connect voice-to-voice in real time with an office-bound mate. Every so often, say no to text or email, and make that call. This can zap some precious time. I know this because, since I work solitary so much of the time, I personally find that I start jabbering away once I start a phone conversation. I barely realize my thirst for someone to talk to until the conversation gets rolling.

I hang up energized. That time genuinely builds fellowship and friendship and keeps you in the loop with office happenings in a way a typed note simply can't.

I fancy myself a borderline introvert (although friends disagree). I enjoy the quiet of my home and my own company (with Zena, my dog), but I admit I miss the connecting, friendships, and chances to meet new people in an office—those things rarely happen when you work from home. Even when you go in for meetings, you never quite get that.

6. **To work remotely, you must be hired as a remote worker.** Not so. When I conducted research for my book *Love Your Job: The New Rules for Career Happiness,* as well as interviews with hundreds of

workers, I discovered a humble truth: that more flexibility in scheduling day-to-day activities leads to greater happiness on the job, and an increasing number of workers were negotiating for that wiggle room with their managers.

You *can* convince your boss that it's time for them to join the trend and let you, too, work from home. Here's how:

Do your prep.

First, you may have already been working remotely due to the COVID-19 stay-at-home mandate where you live. So have some mojo. Take stock of your previous telecommuting performance and recognize that you're solidly prepared for the arrangement.

Show, don't tell. When you're out of sight, your boss wants to know he or she can trust you. If you've been working from home the last few months, pull together a record of your projects completed on time, or ahead of schedule. List new business landed, say, or any other measure that allows your boss to get a bead on how you met the challenges of working remotely and the results.

Tout your digital communication skills. You must have a good handle on all aspects of communicating to managers, clients, and your team of co-workers via video chats and file sharing. Whether it's Slack messaging, Zoom, Skype video meetings, or a using a collaboration app like Google Docs, seamless communication is expected.

Have employees from your company worked from home in the past? Did they work partially or fully remotely? Is your job appropriate for remote work? These answers are essential to find out before you start plotting out your plan. If no one from your company has ever worked remotely, you might have a more challenging sell to your boss.

If you know colleagues who work from home, ask them how it's going, and what challenges they have with it. What's the upside? How did they ask the boss if they could work from home either full-time or part-time?

Plan your remote work "ask" with your boss.

Don't wing it. Write out a precise proposal beforehand that covers every nitty-gritty detail of how you'll telecommute, including the number of hours you'll work from home, when you'll be in the office to work or attend meetings, and how you'll factor in unanticipated overtime.

You must be able to articulate how having the flexibility to work from home will make you more efficient. It will remove a long commute, for example, and allow you more time on the job. Increased productivity is one reason employers are often eager to let employees work remotely.

Time your remote working pitch.

You might slip in your request to your manager during a routine performance review or a scheduled meeting about your career objectives. But, in my opinion, it deserves its own standalone meeting.

And that takes some preparation. It's hard to know in advance when your boss will be having a decent day (and potentially be more open to contemplating your proposal). But there are classic clues to when it's a good time to have the "work from home conversation," and when it isn't—it just takes some research. For instance, is your department facing cutbacks? Is your boss's boss putting on pressure to raise the bar on their game, or is there a big project nearing a deadline? If so, you might need to cool your heels and wait until things are less stressful.

Stay focused on who wins. Hint: It's not about you.

Don't put your appeal in terms of how you will benefit from working from home. (I'll be less stressed, I can spend less time commuting, I can spend more time with family.) Even though these are all essential to bring up at some stage, as I mentioned previously, the crux of the conversation must be about how it will be an advantage to your boss and how your employer will profit. You'll be a more productive worker, for example, or there will be more time for you to work on nights and weekends if the position demands that.

Your opening salvo to your boss: "I'd like to explore the opportunity to work from home and how you and the department can benefit."

Keep your expectations in check.

Once workers have returned to the office, having an employee ask if they can work from home may be new terrain for your boss. And their gut reaction is often that you might not work as hard, might be less accessible, or might be unable to collaborate with your team on the spur of the moment. By nature, bosses tend to worry about not being able to control what you do with your time and to keep tabs on your whereabouts. This feeling of powerlessness may be subconscious, but that reaction is simply human nature.

It's your job to be able to quash these qualms. Rather than asking if you can immediately transition to fully remote work, take it one step at a time. This could be through a three- to six-month trial period, or through a shift to working from home one or two days per week. After this probationary period, you can go back and assess how working from home is going for both of you.

During that trial period, interaction and communication will be the key to your success, so you need to stay connected and open about any obstacles, either on your part or from your boss's perspective, that need to be dealt with immediately. The pilot period is a precarious one. So use that time to show your boss that you're up to the task of working from home—and that as you previously told him or her, it will make you more productive.

For me, my friends, and colleagues who also work at home, deciding when to get our jobs done—whether it's 5 a.m. or 10 p.m.—makes us feel more in charge, more alive, and more engaged.

Show, don't tell.

Give it time to roll out.

There may be a gap between when you make the first ask to your boss and when you fully change over into the work-from-home schedule that you have in mind. Many compromises and tweaks may need to be made along the way. So take things one step at a time. Your best argument for working from home, of course, is a great performance—wherever you do your work.

Consider hiring a remote coach to help you.
Not surprisingly, there are career coaches who offer this subset of training. Virtual Work Insider (virtualworkinsider. com), for instance, is a firm started by Sacha Connor, who pioneered virtual work at The Clorox Company. While Connor's firm primarily works with companies to build strategies and personalized coaching to train their managers to lead remote teams, the firm also provides coaching to help workers create a plan to convince managers to let them work remotely.

Negotiating tip: In a recent study by Stanford University, researchers found that when employees worked from home, their productivity significantly increased. The time they usually spent chitchatting with co-workers, commuting to and from work, and taking breaks was now used to embrace a focused, full workday. You might mention this finding to your manager.

A Flex-Time Checklist

- Talk to your manager or HR department to see if your company has a formal policy for allowing flexible schedules.
- Talk to co-workers you know who have a flexible arrangement to get their opinion of the pros and cons.
- Draft a plan that defines what your work schedule would be, the number of hours you would work, how unplanned overtime would be treated, how often you would check in with an office visit, and other issues.
- Request a trial period of three to six months so both you and your boss can see how the plan works out and fine-tune it if necessary.

7. **You're on your own.** When you work remotely, true, you may miss out on the brainstorming synergy you get from simply being in the room or a meetup in the elevator.

More subtly, you can't read body language during a conference meeting if you're calling in from a remote location. Just seeing your colleagues virtually may prevent you from understanding what's really going on.

But you really don't have to be alone. And thanks to advancements in technology, that's rapidly changing, with audio and visual Gotomeeting, Skype, Zoom, and Google chats taking over as the preferred way to have virtual meetings. Plus, the almost-like-being-there workplace instant messaging through Slack really does help you feel the love of being part of a team.

What people tend to miss most about working in an office are spur-of-the-moment poke-your-head-in visits. Smart use of technology like the apps mentioned above makes up some of that difference, though. I know one remote manager, for example, who recently ran a "virtual baby shower" for one of her team members.

And again, the phone really doesn't weigh a ton. "I often opt for a phone call rather than an email," says a pal who's a telecommuting IBM sales executive. "I know not everyone appreciates the time zap, but I preface it by saying: 'It's a quick question.'" She thinks phone calls result in more honest responses than she'd get with emails. I agree with her.

8. **Work-from-home jobs are usually starter positions.** This statement is far from the truth. Take a look back at the remote employer section. You'll discover that jobs recently posted run the gamut from entry-level to senior positions that require decades of experience and specialized training. Among the most common telecommute job titles these days are account manager, accountant, business development manager, engineer, program manager, and project manager, according to FlexJobs research. In fact, it is increasingly common for companies to offer a remote option for high-level jobs such as corporate attorney and senior-level web developer.

C H A P T E R

The Nuts and Bolts of Your Remote Job Search

Landing a remote job requires a bit of the old soft-shoe to assure the hiring manager, and ultimately your boss, that you've been down this road before (or at least have the character for it) and are prepared for the arrangement.

You've done this before. Front and center, showcase your previous telecommuting experience in your cover letter, résumé, and during interviews. If you have not held a position beforehand that let you telecommute, stress skills you hold, such as your ability to communicate effectively over the phone, via email, and on video conferences. Tout your self-motivation, your ease with technology, and your solid time-management skills.

Do the digital dance. Promoting your technical skills, of course, is vital at each touch point with a potential employer. If you don't have these in your wheelhouse, I advise adding them tout de suite. You must have a good handle on all aspects of communicating to managers, clients, and your team of co-workers via video chats and file sharing. It helps if you're also comfortable troubleshooting if a computer glitch appears.

Things change quickly in the tech world, but staying current will demonstrate that you're a feasible candidate. That goes a long way in easing an employer's concerns that you might get tripped up communicating from a remote location.

In fact, I know of instances when a candidate who was less qualified than another for a position, but was nimble with the tools to make remote working seamless, got the offer over the less tech-savvy one. Employers want you to hit the ground running with as little hand-holding as possible. It can help to have a recently added online course or certification on your résumé that shows that you're ready and able.

Recognize the Skills Remote Employers Value

Tech Tools You Need to Know

You can develop your digital collaboration abilities by familiarizing yourself with common tools and software used to link remote employees together, including:

- Common applications for sharing work files: Google Drive, Dropbox, and Box (box.com).
- Videoconferencing apps: Zoom (zoom.us), BlueJeans (bluejeans.com), Skype (skype.com), and WebEx (webex.com).
- Email and texting apps: Slack (slack.com) messaging and Microsoft Teams (products.office.com/en-us/microsoft-teams/group-chat-software) are now the preferred ways of instant messaging for many employers for you to "work remotely without feeling remote," as Microsoft says on its website.
- Collaboration apps for team projects include Basecamp (basecamp.com), Asana (asana.com), and Trello (trello.com/en-US).
- Common communication apps are Skype, Zoom, Slack, and Chatter (salesforce.com/products/chatter/overview).
- Google's office apps suite include, Google Docs for writing and Google Sheets for spreadsheets.

Polish your skills in advance. Remote-work digital training is available on online-learning sites such as LinkedIn Learning (linkedin.com/learning/me), Coursera (coursera.org), Udemy (udemy.com), and YouTube (youtube.com). LinkedIn Learning, for example, has 16 free courses on productively working remotely for success. Go to linkedinlearning.com and search under "remote work." LinkedIn Learning and Microsoft Learn are also now offering free skills training for in-demand jobs.

The app developers themselves provide free online tutorials: Microsoft's on-demand end-user training videos for Teams, Slack (slack.com/resources/slack-101) tutorial, Zoom's instructor-led weekly online training classes (zoom.us/livetraining), and free video lessons for adult learners that Google offers for its office apps suite, including Docs, Sheets, and Slides (applieddigitalskills.withgoogle.com/en/digital-training).

Hit the classroom or sign up for online training courses at your local community college.

Workplaceless (workplaceless.com) has a remote-work certification course ($195). The full course covers seven topics, including workflow and time management, teams, and communication.

Some nonprofits also offer digital skills training for older workers who can't afford classes. These include Senior Planet (seniorplanet.org) and Senior Service America (seniorserviceamerica.org), which runs programs to connect low-income and disadvantaged adults with prospective employers.

If you familiarize yourself with these applications before applying for remote jobs, add that to your LinkedIn profile, résumé, and cover letters. This clearly demonstrates to a potential employer that you're up to date in software that might have cost them time and money to train you.

Skills, Skills, Skills

Employers look for skills in two groups: hard skills and soft skills. Hard skills are those mandatory to do the job, such as network security, accounting, programming, marketing, data analysis, and graphic design. These skills are typically learned and are quantifiable; for example, you can earn a degree or certification or at least point to a course on a transcript showing that you received training in a specific area. Or you can point to jobs you held in the past that required those same skills. Soft skills are more individual and harder to measure, such as the abilities to communicate clearly, solve problems, manage your own time, and be a team player.

Find out Which Hard Skills Are Required

Nearly every position, both remote and in-house, requires certain hard skills. I can't possibly cover them all, because they can be highly specific for certain positions.

Employers make this pretty easy to get a bead on through the job descriptions they post. Review the ones that interest you and make a list. Which ones do you have already? Which ones would make sense to add? Which ones would be nice—but not essential—to have in order to get hired?

Following are a few broad skill sets that remote employers look for in nearly every field:

Technology skills: As I mentioned above, employers expect remote employees to be comfortable with a range of technological applications.

Data analytics: Some of the fastest-growing occupations are information security analysts, operations research analysts, and statisticians, according to the Bureau of Labor Statistics (BLS). This means that candidates with a strong background in data science and analytics will have a real advantage in the job market. Smart employers are looking for people who grasp data and its significance to a business.

You might need a brushup or a step-up. For example, if you're seeking a job as a business analyst, advanced Excel courses can help, or maybe you're a graphic designer and need to sharpen your skills using Adobe Illustrator, Photoshop, InDesign, and Illustrator.

These skills can often be added via an online offering. A great place to check up on online courses is *U.S. News & World Report* (usnews.com/education/online-education/articles/us-news-ranks-best-online-programs), which ranks the best online programs each year.

Time Management

When you work from home, a huge key to making it a success is managing your time with a disciplined approach to planning prowess. Your success comes down to how well you can prioritize your work demands. There's no wiggle room for being late with a project deadline or jumping on a conference call. That demands some mental prep.

Numerous tools and strategies can assist you in managing your time more efficiently:

- You can tap a tool like Toggl (toggl.com), a productivity time-tracker tool.
- Evernote (evernote.com), a free note-taking app, helps you capture and organize ideas, projects, and to-do lists. You can record your meetings and track how much time you spend on certain tasks.
- Trello (trello.com) is another popular app that lets you create columns for "to do," "in progress," "completed," and much more.
- Microsoft To Do is a task management app that helps manage projects and much more. It includes a personalized daily planner. You can set one-time or recurring due dates and reminders from bills to meetings.

You might also opt, like I do, to go the old-fashioned route and use a wall calendar or a paper day planner binder to list your upcoming assignments and personal to-dos as well, and check them off as you finish. Nothing makes me happier than this simple, physical act. I do, however, set up visual reminders for virtual meetings to pop up on my MacBook Air screen each morning, and I make sure all incoming electronic invitations are uploaded there. I also set an alarm on my iPhone to alert me shortly before I have a virtual meeting or call scheduled.

Recognizing the Soft Skills Employers Value

Soft skills may seem simple, but stay with me. A biggie is, of course, your attitude, which is a measure of how effortlessly and capably you'll work and collaborate with your co-workers, your manager, and perhaps the employer's customers.

Here are the softer skills I'm talking about, organized in alphabetical order. Rate yourself and check areas where you may need upgrading. Then ratchet it up in those areas, if you can.

- *Analytical thinking:* Employers want people who think logically, can size up situations, seek additional information when necessary, and make fact-based decisions.

- *Balance.* It's easy to get lost in your work and overdo it, or slack off from time to time to run an errand or two when no one's looking. You must draw the line between your work and your home life.
- *Communication* (oral and written): Employers value remote workers who communicate well both orally and through the written word. When you're a good communicator, you generally relate better with co-workers, managers, clients, customers, vendors, and others.
- *Confidence:* Being confident means you can take initiative without the continuous need for approval.
- *Cooperation:* Success on a remote job demands a capability and a willingness to be a team player and to get along and collaborate with others, including co-workers, managers, vendors, clients, and customers.
- *Creativity:* Even in noncreative jobs, you're expected to be able to think creatively to adapt to shifting conditions and resolve problems.
- *Curiosity:* The desire to learn is a magic ingredient that employers look for in an employer.
- *Flexibility:* Most employers I have canvassed never fail to mention that they truly value an employee who can adjust quickly. You need to be able to shift effortlessly from one project to another. You also must be open to logging the extra hours when needed and to balance assignments.
- *Honesty and integrity:* These qualities are essential in building trust. As an employee, even if you aren't in the office, you're a reflection of the organization and its values when you're on the phone or a video chat.
- *Learning:* Employers are attracted to workers who push themselves to learn new things and ways of doing things and are curious about adding new skills and knowledge.
- *Listening:* This is a big piece of having great communication skills. You need to be able to hear, process, and act on instructions. When you're not front and center with someone, this can take some focus and attention so you can solve a problem or complete a task. Importantly, it can go a long way toward not misinterpreting an email or a written message. We all know how easy that can be when you misread the tone.

The Editors of Fortune magazine asked 15 top business leaders to name the personality trait that they think has fueled their success. One answer: "A focus on effective communication—and it all starts with the ability to really listen," says Lockheed Martin CEO Marillyn Hewson. Take this insight to heart.

- *Patience:* Many jobs are nerve-wracking and hectic at times. Employers are counting on you to be calm and cool, especially if you have a position that is customer facing and dependent on the trust and rapport you create.
- *People skills:* As we discussed in Chapter 4, "Work-from-Home Myths," remote work is not really for introverts. Your capacity to connect with others and build working relationships is extremely important.
- *Positive attitude:* Upbeat and energetic employees make your manager's job easier, and the truth is that it makes you more engaged in your work, too.
- *Reliability:* Reliability simply means keeping your promise, and when you agree to work remotely for someone, that's an assurance to do your job 100 percent of the time.
- *Resilience:* The ability to bounce back from setbacks is vital for success.
- *Resourcefulness:* Resourcefulness is gauged by what you can accomplish with what you're given. No excuses.
- *Self-management:* This is the defining quality for a remote worker. Employers will expect you to stay on track and get the job done professionally.

Examining Your Skills

I urge you to make your own list of skills that will be useful when writing your résumé, filling out job applications, and prepping for interviews.

1. Write down formal education you received that has given you a work skill, such as coding, nursing, or accounting.
2. Include any other work-related courses, seminars, or workshops you participated in.

3. List any licenses or certifications you've attained.
4. Jot down any capabilities you have in other areas, such as fluency in a second language or public speaking.
5. List all office software you can work with. This includes spreadsheet applications, presentation programs, database management software, desktop publishing or graphics programs, blogging platforms, and so on.
6. Review your soft skills.

You may not realize skills you possess until others call attention to them. Ask friends, families, and colleagues for some feedback. Don't limit yourself to skills you learned at work. If you worked pro bono as treasurer for your local parent-teacher organization, for example, you have proficiency with financial management and budgeting. If you raised children, you have an understanding of scheduling. If you cared for an aging relative, you may have been a financial manager, hiring manager, patient advocate, and project manager. How you grew your skills is less essential than having the skills that meet an employer's requirements.

Tip: The U.S. Department of Labor's CareerOneStop has a Skills Profiler (careerinfonet.org/skills) that generates a list of skills in several categories based on the job type and work activities you specify.

Redeploying Skills

Although you may need supplementary training to pick up a new remote job, especially if it is also a career change, many skills are exchangeable—you're using them in a different way or in a fresh situation. The ability to manage projects, for example, is a transferrable skill.

Where to Find Remote Jobs

You can find legitimate jobs on these sites that focus on remote work. Unless otherwise indicated, they don't charge job seekers. In addition to these sites geared specifically to remote jobs, the big job boards such as AARP's job board (jobs.aarp.org/),

CareerBuilder.com, Glassdoor.com, Indeed.com, and Monster.com are searchable for "remote" positions. Type in the word "remote" in the search box that asks for what job title you are looking for and you can drill down from there. On a recent visit to Monster, for example, more than 62,000 remote jobs popped up.

- **FlexJobs.com** includes remote work from home and other flexible jobs in over 50 career categories and ranging from entry-level to executive. A monthly subscription costs $14.95.
- **Fiverr** (fiverr.com) has over 250 freelance categories.
- **Freelancer.com** connects employers and freelancers globally. Areas range from software development to writing, data entry and design to engineering, the sciences, sales and marketing, accounting and legal services.
- **Jobspresso.co** is a Canada-based site, frequented by U.S. workers, focused on remote jobs.
- **The National Telecommuting Institute** (ntiathome.org/), a nonprofit that works with the Social Security Administration to fill telecommuting jobs with people who have disabilities,
- **Ratracerebellion.com** has been at the forefront of the work-from-home revolution since 1999.
- **Remote.co**, founded by the woman who created FlexJobs, offers a great Q&A section to learn about leading remote-forward companies lists.
- **Sidehusl.com** is a user-friendly site that researches, reviews, and rates more than 300 online platforms geared to job opportunities. Hit what work you want to do, and it shows you the possibilities.
- **SkipTheDrive.com** is devoted to full- and part-time telecommuting jobs.
- **Toptal** (toptal.com) Toptal is a network of the top freelance software developers, designers, finance experts, product managers, and project managers from around the world.
- **UpWork** (upwork.com) has millions of jobs posting annually with seventy categories of work.
- **VirtualVocations.com** offers limited access to the site's job listings for free. Full access costs $15.99 monthly.

- **Work At Home Vintage Experts** (wahve.com) is a contract staffing firm that places older professionals in work-from-home jobs currently in the insurance, accounting, and human resource fields.
- **WeWorkRemotely.com** includes programming, sales, and other jobs.
- **Working Nomads** (Workingnomads.co/jobs) lists tech, management, marketing, and other jobs.
- **Ziprecruiter.com** lists over 8 million jobs, searchable by categories such as work from home, part-time remote, stay-at-home mom, work-from-home RN, and more.

WHAT A REMOTE JOB POST LOOKS LIKE

In February, as tax season began, on the job board Glassdoor, the financial software firm Intuit had a posting for a **Remote Credentialed Tax Professional** to work in a seasonal, virtual, customer-facing role using Intuit's video communication software (SmartLook) to interact with customers.

Other qualifications, roles, and skills

- Help TurboTax customers who are working on their tax return with tax advice, product/software inquiries, and tax calculations.
- An ability to create high-quality customer interactions and experiences that instill confidence using deep customer empathy, and your deep knowledge and expertise in the field of tax preparation.
- Utilize and leverage government websites, professional resources, and team expertise to seek out and deliver the right answer to the customer using everyday language.
- Apply defined practices, procedures, and company policies to troubleshoot and resolve tax advice and preparation customer inquiries. Document customer interactions.
- Must possess active, unrestricted credentials: EA (Enrolled Agent), CPA (Certified Public Accountant), or Practicing Attorney with strong tax preparation experience and extensive knowledge of tax laws.
- Must possess active PTIN (Preparer Tax Identification Number).
- 3 or more years of recent experience preparing federal and state individual 1040 tax returns for clients/customers, using commercial tax preparation software.

C H A P T E R

Crafting Your Résumé and Cover Letter

No matter what stage of your working life you're in, creating a résumé can be daunting. How do you accurately and creatively share your skills and experience in a one-dimensional presentation? I'm a big fan of LinkedIn profiles where the language isn't stiff, and you can post videos and share presentations to build a full picture of who you are.

But in the job search process, a résumé has not gone out of style and is still your calling card for the official record.

I recently had to write my own résumé for a job opportunity that sounded intriguing, after not having done so in more than 20 years! Trust me, it was tricky. I asked my niece, 28, who had just landed a great job after graduate school, to send me her most recent one to get the latest in formatting. I had my sister edit it for me. It was not a pleasant experience.

I kept reminding myself of all the advice I share for jobseekers who ask me for help and, step-by-step, I did it. So here goes.

As I mentioned above, remote job seekers must shine a light on any telecommuting, freelance gigs, and work-from-home jobs you've performed in the past, or still do. This demonstrates to potential employers that you know the drill. You have the self-discipline, time-management savvy, and tech know-how to perform from the get-go.

Your résumé is your highlight sizzle reel. It's your advertisement, not your obituary.

Ten Ways Your Résumé Can Capture a Hiring Manager's Consideration

The more experience you have, the harder it can be to create a résumé that's concise and truly conveys your expertise.

The challenge is to grab someone's attention straight away, a requirement that's increasingly important now that the hiring process for most jobs starts digitally. Once the résumé you upload for a job posting gets to a human resource manager, 39 percent of them spend less than a minute initially looking at it, according to a survey from CareerBuilder. Nearly 1 in 5 (19 percent) spend less than 30 seconds.

Here are ten smart ways to make certain that your résumé gets noticed:

1. **Start like LinkedIn.** A résumé is your stage to shout out your skills, accomplishments, and strengths. Instead of a dull boilerplate objective, begin with a personal statement. According to Beverly Jones, an executive career coach and author of *Think Like an Entrepreneur, Act Like a CEO*, "Done properly, this statement, or summary, of who you are can pull someone in fast."

   This method of launching your résumé is a nod to the popularity of LinkedIn. "LinkedIn has changed the way many hiring managers read résumés now," Jones said. "They expect this more personal approach."

   Be bold and write this section in the first person, as you would your LinkedIn Summary statement. This should be a quick roll call of your triumphs and skill set in the same language you would use when talking to someone.

   For instance, you might describe the most important thing you've accomplished recently in your career, what you enjoy most about the work you do, something you are really proud of, or how your skills have allowed you to contribute to the success of your previous employers' missions and bottom lines. The subtle message: You have the chops to help the company meet its objectives.

Keep it tight, say five or six sentences, and end with a bulleted list, such as "Areas of Concentration," with roughly three examples.

And in your desire to super-sell yourself, don't get carried away. Three-fourths of human resources managers report having caught a lie on a résumé, according to CareerBuilder.

2. **Use your keywords.** The idea of having a one-and-done résumé is a relic of the past. Your résumé should be customized for each position you are considering. Use as much of the job posting's language as possible. If your résumé doesn't contain exactly the right keywords that appear in a job posting, when you send it electronically, it may not make it through an employer's applicant tracking system (ATS).

For example, if the employer asks for "strong Excel and report-writing skills," tuck these keyword expressions in your skills section and somewhere in the narrative of your past work experience. If the firm is looking for a "sales associate" with "a strong customer focus," then include this phrase two or three times, or if the job requires someone who has "managed" a team, use "managed," not "directed" or "operated," or any other synonym.

Tools like Jobscan (jobscan.co) can also help you compare your résumé against job descriptions and analyze which keywords you need to include.

3. **Simplify your fonts and format.** Keep it to two pages. In some situations, it can be three pages, but only make your résumé as long as it needs to be to underscore your credentials. Select a font that's modern and easy on the eyes. I recommend Arial, Helvetica, or Calibri. Stick to a 10- to 14-point size, and use black type against white paper for the body of the résumé. Your name, however, might be in 15-point size, all caps; your contact information and section heads might be in 12. But be consistent in the formatting, and use boldface type, italics, and underlining sparingly.

Prepare the document in a plain Microsoft Word document format that can be viewed easily on most computers. You will also use this version to print out as a hard copy or to upload into an online job application form. Most job postings state what type of format is preferred. Some employers or job boards will require a pdf format. I suggest having one master version in a doc format that you can easily customize for each individual job.

Put your contact information at the top of the résumé: your first and last name, email address, phone number (just one), a customized LinkedIn URL, and a website, if you have one. Including your LinkedIn URL and blog or website address makes it easy for recruiters and hiring managers to find out more about you online. List the city and state in which you live. Omit your street address for privacy reasons.

4. **Spotlight your skills.** Most job seekers use the traditional chronological or reverse-chronological résumé format. But I recommend highlighting your specific skills first, focusing on those that are most transferable to the job you're looking for. More than a third of human resource managers (37 percent) said they preferred having skills listed first on a résumé, according to the CareerBuilder report.

Focusing on the skills relevant to the job you're applying for up high delivers the "why you should hire me" message before you start cataloging previous jobs. After all, what you can do for them today is what an employer really wants to know. And if you're looking to change careers, or have a gap in your work history, it's even more critical to focus on your skills, not your positions.

The top three or four key broad skill categories mandatory for the job you're targeting will help you to pick what to include in this section. Add recent training, education, and certifications to emphasize your professional development and willingness to learn.

In the next section, present your professional experience in reverse chronological order, starting with your most recent position. Include the following details for each organization you served: start and end dates (month and year); organization's name, location, and what the organization does or did; position(s) you held; and major accomplishments at each position.

Include volunteer positions or internships in this section— related experience doesn't just have to be paid positions. I advise including any volunteer work that suggests you have management skills. Being in charge of a gala fundraising event, for instance, converts to sales and marketing chops. Holding a board position shows leadership capability.

5. **Weave a story.** As you describe your experience, remember the basics of a good story are *who, what, where, when, why,* and *how.* No one wants to know just what tasks you performed. They want to know why it mattered.

Numbers, statistics, and percentages can get attention if you put them in bold type. These are quantifiable results that no one can quibble with when you're touting why you're a good hire. You want to say, for instance, that you grew sales by 25 percent, or you completed a job three months ahead of schedule. Résumé-writing pros refer to this as telling your "CAR story," which stands for "challenge, action, and result."

In your CAR story for each job on your résumé, write about a problem you faced, what you did to solve it, and the specific tangible results of your efforts. For example, "Interviewed machine operators and developed multimedia training programs that reduced training time for new hires by 20 percent." Statements like this show rather than tell. Let reviewers hear your voice and pride in your achievements. Importantly, make sure the CAR stories are relevant to the job for which you are applying.

6. **Be sure to cherry-pick your professional experience.** What employers want to see is your most recent 10 to 15 years of experience. No one wants, or needs, to read every one of your job entries over a four- to five-decade career. Bundle your earlier experiences into one tidy paragraph at the end of your résumé's "experience" section, and skip dates. Only use the work history that's germane to the job you're applying for now.

7. **Don't use full sentences.** Begin with verbs. Get creative. Most résumé bullet points start with the same overused words such as "led" or "managed." "Managed company tax reporting, finance, invoicing, purchasing," for example.

Here are some alternative verbs to consider for various situations, from being in charge of an initiative to saving your employer money to managing, improving, or researching duties:

- Administered
- Advanced
- Advocated
- Amplified
- Analyzed
- Authorized
- Boosted
- Built
- Chaired
- Charted

- Consolidated
- Controlled
- Coordinated
- Created
- Critiqued
- Customized
- Delivered
- Designed
- Developed
- Devised
- Educated
- Engineered
- Enhanced
- Evaluated
- Executed
- Expedited
- Founded
- Implemented
- Influenced
- Launched
- Mentored
- Mobilized
- Negotiated
- Orchestrated
- Outpaced
- Outperformed
- Partnered
- Produced
- Recruited
- Redesigned
- Spearheaded
- Tested
- Transformed
- Verified

8. **Mind the gaps.** It's best to have a good experience to sub for periods you were not working such as being able to say you traveled, performed community service, added a degree, or pursued other education. Include a one-line explanation, such as "Volunteered

for Habitat for Humanity," to fill in for any extended periods of unemployment.

If you were out of the workforce for caregiving duties, you can hawk that, too. You were a "project manager," managing a team of other caregivers, from nurses and doctors to physical therapists. You were a "researcher" tracking down the best doctors and medical care. You may have been a "financial manager" in charge of bill paying and insurance claims. Use action verbs to portray your caregiving experience: directed, enabled, facilitated, hired, supervised, controlled, coordinated, navigated, negotiated, secured, and resolved.

9. **Add some punch.** Interests, hobbies, activities, and professional memberships can also help you get noticed. That can be a great way to subtly deflect an employer's opinion that older workers don't have the stamina for the job. It might even provide a personal connection to someone who is reading your résumé, if he or she shares a similar passion.

10. **Hit delete.** Eliminate college or high school graduation dates. Remove jobs that lasted less than six months. Avoid quirky job titles; the title could jettison you from a recruiter's search criteria. "Wordsmith," for instance, is unlikely to show up in an ATS search for the specific keyword "editor." Skip "References available upon request." Of course they are.

Hiring a Pro to Help

It's hard to brag about yourself, and the sheer mechanics of composing the details can be exasperating and time-consuming. There is help to be had here. Ask for it.

If you're a college graduate, check with your college career center to see whether it offers free résumé services. Another option is to seek the assistance of a career counselor, coach, or consultant to help you write your résumé as well as hone your job search skills and strategies.

LinkedIn has a "Profinder" feature (linkedin.com/profinder/résumé-writing) that suggests résumé writers who can help you. You can receive free quotes from potential writers via the site's matchmaking service after you fill in a short form that describes your needs, such as that you are looking for help with a traditional résumé or your LinkedIn profile.

Here are a few professional résumé services you might explore: AvidCareerist (avidcareerist.com), Career Trend (careertrend.net), Chameleon Résumés (chameleonresumes.com), Executive Career Brand (executivecareerbrand.com), and Great Resumes Fast (greatresumesfast.com).

AARP Resume Advisor offers a free expert review. Members get discounted pricing on having "an expertly written and keyword-optimized resume" starting at $119. Toss in the cover letter for a fee of $159.

You can also find certified résumé writers through Career Directors International (careerdirectors.com) or the National Résumé Writers Association (thenrwa.com). Fees range from $300 to $1,500 or more. You can probably deduct the cost of preparing and mailing your résumé from your federal taxes.

At the very minimum, proofread your résumé. Ask someone you trust to double-check it for you. As I said, I asked my older sis. I recommend reading it out loud, too. For me, that's the single best way to catch missed words and grammatical gaffes.

Writing a Killer Cover Letter

The impact of the cover letter fluctuates by company. Lots of employers skip the cover letter and depend on automated systems to process résumés and pair candidates to their job needs.

But don't be fooled into thinking this is the new reality. There are still those out there, particularly smaller businesses and start-ups, that rely on the cover letter to pull the lid off and look a little closer at your written communication ability. It is the gateway for your résumé.

I recommend that unless the job posting says don't do it, always include a cover letter with your résumé. A well-written cover letter instantly represents who you are and what you bring to the table that is relevant to the employer's needs.

A cover letter can be the place to recount your work story and is often more valuable than a résumé in doing so, if you're transitioning to a new field.

To be realistic, the real power of the cover letter comes into play when you get to the interview stage. It helps your potential interviewer learn more about you. If you don't pair it with your résumé when you apply electronically, send it along to the person who is interviewing you ahead of time.

Writing a Career-Change Cover Letter

It is critical that these covers letters are short, snappy, and to the point. If you're making this career transition, you need to be very upfront about your "why."

I recommend making the reason for your transition very clear within the first paragraph of your career change cover letter.

Here are some questions to answer within your cover letter:

- Why are you making this transition?
- What is it about this job/field that you enjoy?
- Why this particular employer?
- How can you help this employer succeed with your current skill set?
- What are you selling?
- What can you bring to their party to make them successful? Why?

Don't apply willy-nilly. When you're career transitioning, you're not reinventing yourself; you're redeploying the skills that you already have built up.

You need to highlight why your present skill set is as pertinent to this new field as it was to your old field. Most importantly, you need to enthusiastically express why bringing your skills to that team will allow it to succeed because, in the end, it's always about the employer's goals, not your own.

Writing a killer cover letter is a key step in the job search dance. I truly believe this. While not every employer accepts one in this era of automated résumé processing, for many it's what first piques interest in a candidate. So unless the job posting states otherwise or you're submitting your résumé on a site that includes no option for a cover letter, always include one.

View it as your opening act. Make it concise and confident. You have just a few sentences to demonstrate how well you understand the needs of the organization and, importantly, how well you communicate that knowledge in writing. Hard to believe, but according to CareerBuilder.com, 45 percent of job seekers don't include a cover letter. So don't be one of them. Take your time and create a letter in which each word works magic for you.

Here are my do's and don'ts:

Do your homework. Start by reading the job description with a sharp eye. Learn as much as you can about the industry and your prospective employer. Visit the company's website and the sites of the company's top competitors. Visit the job-hunt site Glassdoor.com and do a Google search to dig up additional information. Find out who your supervisor is likely to be and look up the person on LinkedIn.

All this will help you craft a customized letter for this particular job that's addressed to the person who'll interview you or make the decision.

Do some soul-searching. If you've found something about the company that truly speaks to a cause and interest that you care about, this is your moment to put that front and center.

Keep it brief. Your letter should be no longer than one page. Think of it as a written version of your elevator speech: a short, snappy summary of who you are and what kind of job you'd like to find. It's a sales pitch you will tap again and again as you network and interview your way to your next position.

Organize. A good cover letter typically has three sections. The first is the introduction. In the opening paragraph, tell the employer what job you're applying for and mention the exact title and position as it appears in the job post, if there is one.

Explain why you're applying for it and (if applicable) who referred you or how you heard about it. Employers like to hire people they know or people whom they know actually know of.

For example: "My friend and former colleague, Joanne Smith, told me you're looking for a detail-oriented person with years of experience in strategic communication. That is precisely what I can offer, and the opening is timed perfectly for my decision to pursue my goal of working for [organization name]."

Second, briefly describe your skills in a way that matches them to the needs of the organization. Remember, job hunting is never about you. It's about what you can do for the employer. Highlight training, education, and skills that are particularly relevant to the position and

146

the organization's needs. Be specific without going into too much detail. Think of your letter as a carefully planned appetizer that whets the reader's appetite for the main course—your résumé.

In the last section, refer to the résumé and express eagerness to meet with the person. For example: "For additional details, please see my résumé (attached). I look forward to the opportunity to meet with you in person to discuss the position and my qualifications in greater depth."

Wrap it up with a line that indicates you will follow up with them in the next few days. Invite the person to contact you and include the best phone number and your email.

Always end with: "Thank you for your time and consideration."

Those are the "do's." Now here are some "don'ts," which I've learned from reviewing hundreds of job applications over the years and speaking with dozens of people in human resources.

Don't be generic. Instead, tailor each letter (and résumé) to the specific position.

Don't waste space. Phrases such as "Let me introduce myself" add little to your message. Get to the point.

Don't be bland. For example: "As was mentioned in the job description for this position, your company is in need of a team-oriented individual with a background of 10 years or more in the fields of marketing and communications, and proficiency with standard office computer applications. As you can see from the details in my résumé, my qualifications make me perfectly suited to that position." Would you want to read that? Better to say something like this: "Your company needs a team player with experience in marketing and communications. I am that person."

Don't merely repeat the contents of your résumé. Instead, highlight your particular skills and achievements.

Don't call attention to your age. This is a big one for older workers. Citing your 30 or 40 years of experience creates a certain impression. Instead, use words such as "extensive" or "significant" to describe your experience.

Don't include your salary requirements. Unless the organization specifically requests this information, save the salary discussion for when you're close to being offered the job.

Finally, fine-tune. Once you've got a "final" draft of your letter, print it and read it closely—but don't send it yet. Revise it to optimize its impact. Here are a few suggestions:

1. Include key words and phrases in your letter that match those used in your résumé, just in case the organization uses an automated system for screening cover letters and résumés.
2. Use bulleted lists to present details. Leaving plenty of white space makes your cover letter more inviting and easier to read.
3. Be clear, direct, and terse. Use short sentences and active verbs.
4. Share your letter with trusted friends who can give you frank reactions. Does your letter feel intriguing? Does it make the reader want to know more about you? If not, revise it.
5. Purge your prose of spelling and grammar errors. Proofread your letter several times and have someone else proofread it as well.

Now you're ready to send it. If you've done it right, the recipient is going to smile and think, "This person sounds fascinating and remarkable—a must-meet!"

CHAPTER

Great Pajama Job Interviews

interviewed for a full-time remote position recently. Yep. I know. Why would I give up running my own business? But a friend had urged me to give it a whirl, arguing that it was a position I would thrive in and the money and benefits were superb. And so I did. I sent off my résumé and cover letter and forgot about it.

True story. It went like this:

Hi Kerry,

Thank you for your interest in opportunities at our company! I received your resume in regards to a position and would like to schedule you for a 30 min Zoom video conference interview with someone from the team. Can you let me know a few dates/times you're available?

Congratulations on moving forward in the process!

She then sent me an email with the name of whom I would be speaking with and the link to the video conference on Zoom.

Feel free to test out the link in advance and let me know if you have any issues!

I tested it out. It allowed me to see if my computer was in the right position (propped up on a few books so the camera was at eye level), what my background looked like, and if I had anything stuck in my teeth. I do a lot of podcasts and video interviews, so I was pretty comfortable with all the stage-setting.

Nonetheless, once the interview started, there were glitches. My interviewer's internet connection was weak and the screen froze twice. I continued chatting away, only to have to repeat it all once she disconnected and logged back in. Exasperating. Finally, I suggested we switch to audio-only. And that worked, but the call took far longer than I had expected and felt disjointed.

In all honesty, it left a bad impression in my mind of the company. I instinctively judged her as being unprofessional for conducting the interview from a location that didn't have a proper internet connection. And the visual image of her squirming around while asking me questions was off-putting.

It was all a reminder that interviewing for a job is a two-way street. You're making decisions on whether you want to work for that employer as much as they are evaluating you.

In today's hiring world, there is a high probability that your first interview will be a virtual one as I experienced. So you need to be prepared.

A good way is to have a friend or partner act as an interviewer and stage a mock interview with Skype or Zoom. You can also simply have someone video you with their smartphone, while you answer the questions they lob your way.

Record it, so you can critique it to see where you can improve your delivery and answers. When you record your interview, you'll be able to evaluate your answers, facial expressions, and body language.

These are two classic questions you can use for your dress rehearsal:

"Why do you want to work at our company?" To ace this query, you have to carefully investigate your potential employer and describe why you're the right one for the job and why the opportunity appeals to you professionally. A solid grasp of the employer's mission can help you formulate your answer.

"What questions do you have for me?" Showing that you are curious and take the process seriously is reflected by your own questions.

I honestly didn't handle this one as smoothly as I should have in my Zoom interview. I had run out of steam by the time my interviewer arrived at this stage where she wanted my questions. It had been over an hour, and I was already thinking of all the work I had on my plate to do that morning. Plus, I had gone over my questions about the position and the company already with my friends who worked there, and she knew I had done so.

I hesitated and then I told her so. I was pretty sure she wouldn't be able to add anything new for me. Maybe that was dismissive of me. But so be it. I would recommend you don't do what I did. Have your questions handy and toss them out there.

Interviews aren't just about giving the right answers—they're about *asking the right questions.* So take the opportunity to ask meaningful, well-researched questions. This will demonstrate to your interviewer that you did your research, and you're taking the interview process seriously.

SHINING UP YOUR PRESENTATION SKILLS

Although some people are naturals, some jobseekers require training and practice to master the art of the job interview, whether virtual, in person, or by phone. To get the training and practice you need, consider the following options.

Join a Toastmasters club (toastmasters.org). Most meetings consist of about 20 people who meet weekly for an hour or two. Participants practice and learn skills of effective speech: focus, organization, language, vocal variety, and body language. You learn how to focus your attention away from your own anxieties and concentrate on your message and your audience, which goes a long way toward acing an interview.

Take a public speaking course. You can find public speaking courses at your local community college. Most courses cover techniques for managing communication anxiety, speaking clearly, tuning into your body language, and much more.

Sign up for an acting class, or an improvisational comedy workshop. These workshops help you build your confidence and stage presence.

Work with a coach. A good career coach can give you feedback and offer advice to sharpen your presentation. You might find a coach by asking friends, colleagues, and family members who they have worked with that they recommend. The Muse offers a platform called Coach Connect (themuse.com/coaching). And a recap from Chapter 6: Contact your college

---

(continued)

career office if you're a college grad, and ask if they provide career counseling or advice to alumni. Many career offices provide services for life to alumni or may charge a lower fee than you would pay for a private counselor. If not, ask whether they can give you a referral. LinkedIn's ProFinder is another searchable source.

You can find a directory of coaches via the International Coach Federation (coachfederation.org). The organization awards a global credential, which is currently held by thousands of coaches worldwide. ICF-credentialed coaches have met educational requirements, received specific coach training, and achieved a designated number of experience hours, among other requirements. Other helpful sites are the Association of Career Professionals International and the National Career Development Association (ncda.org).

New coaches—who may be very experienced professionals—often are eager to take clients for practically nothing in order to build up hours of experience.

Much of what makes a great interview is intuitive. It's chemistry between two people. Each situation is unique. And regardless of how practiced you are, there's plenty of room for improvement when you're in the hot seat.

Kerry's Road Map to Acing an Interview

Check out the prospective employer. Start by going to its website. The "About" page will typically give you information about history, mission, and people. Read the news or press releases page. Also check the company's LinkedIn and Facebook pages, and follow it on Twitter.

Of course, you don't want to rely totally on what the employer says about itself. Search for it on the Web and set up Google News alerts about it.

Search your LinkedIn network for an inside connection. If someone in your network works for the business, or formerly did, contact that person to find out more and perhaps get the contacts of people in the department you hope to join.

Do a background check on your interviewers. LinkedIn pages and a Google search should provide some personal and professional context. If you can find a point of connection, all the better. Find out where people went to school and worked.

Give yourself a "faith lift." Take time to consider some of the highlights of your work, education, and personal life to date. Ask people you trust to recap some of the skills they associate with you.

Rehearse. Get comfortable answering interview questions. They're likely to include "Tell me about yourself," "What are your strengths and weaknesses," and "Why are you a good fit for the job." You'll need to provide concrete examples of your work. Make a list of points you want to convey and then practice how to raise them if the interviewer doesn't ask about them.

Write down questions to ask about the organization. These questions show you are interested and have drilled down on the things that matter to you and show you've done your legwork on the company.

I encourage you to approach an interview as you would a conversation with someone you want to know better and whom you want to know more about you. Look forward to the interview, not with a sense of anxiety, but with excitement. This is a chance to meet someone new and find out whether you and your potential employer are a good fit. You're potential allies, not adversaries.

Personality Bonus

Depending on what remote job you're pursuing, employers are looking for diverse characteristics, so keep these in mind when you're motivating yourself up for your interviews:

- **Curiosity:** An eagerness to learn new things and find solutions conveys a zeal to learn. Ask questions about the company and its services, products, customers, competition, and so on to validate your natural inquisitiveness.
- **Insight:** An understanding of the business, what it does, how it functions, and what its challenges are helps you exhibit your aptitude to fit in and add value.
- **Engagement:** Your capability to carry on a smart conversation with the interviewers reveals engagement. Listen vigilantly to what they say and reply thoughtfully to show that you heard, comprehended, and are able to frame a pertinent response. Engagement is all about showing that you care.
- **Intellect:** Intelligence never goes out of style, and again, doing your homework prior to the interview can set you up nicely to show this characteristic without even trying. Speaking clearly and using proper English also convey a clear level of intelligence and sophistication.

- **Creativity:** The talent for being imaginative and original in your thinking is a magical component. You may be able to show creativity as you respond to questions, or if given an opportunity to talk about a way you resourcefully solved a problem or met a challenge for a previous employer.
- **Drive and determination:** Can you say grit? Interviewers want to catch a vibe of your whatever-it-takes attitude. Be prepared to discuss circumstances at work or in your personal life when you faced adversity or experienced a setback and overcame it.
- **Efficiency:** How productive are you? A key quality that employers seek is someone who is effective in his or her work with good organization skills.
- **Open-mindedness:** A readiness to try new ways of doing things and a tolerance for taking risks are respected attributes in team members and leaders. When answering questions that call on you to consider a certain option, think about your answer cautiously. No top-of-the-head responses.
- **Passion for the organization:** Interviewers want to see that you admire the company and what it does as much as they do and that you're committed to its success. You can show your passion for the organization by researching it carefully; following it on Facebook, LinkedIn, and Twitter; and mentioning precisely what you like most about the organization during the interview. Be prepared to explain *why* you want to work for the organization and what you can do to help it further its mission.
- **Passion for the job:** Being an engaged employee comes down to loving your work and your job. No employer wants to hire someone who under the surface feels they are accepting a role they feel is beneath them or they're overqualified for, nor do they want to hire someone who treats the position as a holding pattern until they find a job they really want. Talk enthusiastically about the work you do and the work you'd like to do for the organization. Chat about how you want to engage yourself in the job and really make a career out of it.
- **Punctuality:** Employers look for people who are reliable and whom they can count on.
- **Team player:** Ultimately, landing a job often comes down to a hiring manager's gut sense of how well you will play with the

other kids. Someone who is willing and cheerful about chipping in and works easily and collaboratively with others will rise to the top.

Acing the Telephone Interview

To shore up your presentation on a telephone interview for any job, remote or not, here are my top recommendations:

Use a landline phone. Skip scratchy cell phone and VoIP (Voice over Internet Protocol) connections. A landline can provide a better link without the technical snags that may upset you during the interview.

Choose a quiet location. Find a place where you can sit comfortably without disturbances from roommates, dogs barking, background music, and street sirens or horn blowing.

Turn off other phones and mute speakers on your computer. You don't want anything ringing or dinging in the background.

Have a copy of your résumé and the job description within eyesight. You may need to refer to particulars from these documents during the call, but don't recite directly from those written words because reading can sound robotic.

Have paper and pen at hand. Write down notes during your conversation. This process helps you pay close attention to the conversation and keep track of what's been said. This works for me, but not everyone benefits from this process. If it stops your ability to listen closely, skip it. That said, keep these tools close by in case a question or talking point strikes you and you want to be sure to circle back to it later on.

Have a (nonalcoholic) drink nearby. A glass of water is my go-to, but a cup of coffee or tea if you're looking for a little caffeine bump is not a bad idea. This helps with throat clearing and keeps your vocal cords lubricated.

Warm up your voice. And if you haven't said anything in a while, warm up your voice before the phone rings. Do-re-me.

Smile. Trust me, the person on the other end of the phone line can hear a smile over the phone. You'll sound positive and send a sense that you're happy to have the chance to discuss the opening. Smile especially when you answer the phone and say hello, when you discuss about your work and what you're passionate about, and when you ask questions about the employer itself. Put a mirror in front of yourself so you can make sure you're smiling. It's not a vanity thing.

Sit up straight. Posture counts. Stand or sit up straight throughout the call. I favor standing. I think it makes my voice sound stronger and more upbeat. I sometimes walk while the interviewer is talking. Moving gives me energy.

Be ready early. Assume your seat and get comfortable about 10 minutes ahead of time. You don't want to sound rushed.

Answer professionally. When the phone rings, smile and welcome the caller with something like, "Hi, this is [name]." If you know who's calling (from Caller ID), consider following up with "Is this [name]?" Don't try to play that you don't know who's calling, because that can make you sound fake.

Listen before you answer. Pause before you reply to a query. Keep your answers to each question to two minutes or less. Rambling is generally not a good thing. Your interviewer will tune out. And because you can't see the person, it's tempting to fill in any pauses in the conversation, while you wait for them to ask another question. Be patient.

Articulate your words and don't speak too rapidly. Projecting your voice clearly and strongly is fundamental, but you might need to pump the breaks at times. I know when I get excited about a topic my speech really takes off. I have to pay attention to rein it in so I sound a hair more professional. If someone already knows me, it doesn't matter, of course. It's the stranger on the other end of the line who is coming in cold that I need to make an impression on.

Eschew fillers such as "like," "you know," and "um." Use precise language to communicate your thoughts. Remind yourself that short pauses are acceptable and much preferred over fillers that can make you sound less sophisticated. It can take some practice to weed these from your phone conversations, but when you make a mental note of it, you will find yourself catching those fillers ahead of time.

Wind up on a cheery note. If you truly want the remote job, end your conversation by saying, "Thanks for the call. I'm very interested in what we've discussed today. What's the next step?" This is your call to action! In my recent interview, I was told that I could expect to hear back from someone in a few days about the next step: taking a writing test. (Seriously!). And I did.

Acing Your Virtual Interview

Online interviews are swiftly becoming more routine. As it sounds, these involve talking live with an interviewer via Skype, Zoom, or other videoconferencing technology or video-recording responses to questions from a recorded interviewer.

Here are some tips to help you become relaxed with these interview arrangements:

Check your equipment. You'll need a reliable internet connection, a webcam, and a microphone. Most computers and laptops have these built in. But if you are doing a lot of interviews, it might be worth investing in an external USB microphone like high-quality Blue Snowball (around $50) that you can easily plug into your computer. If possible, use an Ethernet cable to connect to the internet and turn off Wi-Fi, so your connection is faster and more reliable. With today's super-fast Wi-Fi connections this isn't always necessary, but depending on your setup, it might be a good move.

Do a backdrop check. Look at what will show behind you. If it's a jumble of books, file folders, and paper piles, or even personal items such as pictures from your vacation, do a sweep. Having a painting, bookcase, or attractive plant in the background is best, but make sure the painting and books are tasteful. You don't want anything to distract from you and your message.

Fine-tune the lighting. You want soft light brightening your face. If your room has a window, face it, or put a lamp on the desk in front of you. Avoid backlit scenarios that put you in a shadow and too much frontlighting that makes you squint.

Test with the interview platform. If it's a live video interview, you may need to download the application software and set up an account. If it's a prerecorded interviewer, you'll receive instructions ahead of time about what's needed to partake.

Reboot your computer. Rebooting guarantees that you're not running applications in the background that may disrupt the interview. Exit any applications set up to run automatically whenever you start your computer.

Adjust your webcam and chair. Position your computer screen so you're in the middle (horizontally) and the top of your head is near the top of the computer screen. You should be looking up slightly at the camera, a position that helps define your chin and subtly conveys a message of strength and confidence.

Do a test run. Practice with a friend or family member on the platform you'll be using or something similar. With Skype, you can record it to review. This also helps with figuring out just how loud you need to talk and how to position the screen and camera lens at the top.

Dress for an in-person interview. Solid colors are best. Avoid white. Don't forget some makeup, even if you're a guy. It takes the shine off your skin.

Have a cheat sheet. Sticky notes on your computer screen can prompt you with talking points you want to be sure to emphasize about your experience and why you're a good fit for the job, as well as questions about the firm and the remote position. Have your résumé and the job description handy, too.

Try your best to look into the camera when talking. This one takes discipline. You'll be tempted to look down at yourself on the screen, or at the interviewer on the screen. Gaze into that tiny camera lens at the top of your computer screen and don't waiver. If you do, it breaks eye contact with the interviewer and creates a choppiness to the interaction. Remember, his or her eyes should be on the tiny camera lens, too.

Smile when applicable. Smiling delivers a big lift for your video charisma and energizes the interview. Try warming up ahead of time by thinking of something funny to make you laugh, or laughing at yourself in a mirror to relax your facial muscles. Smile especially during the meet and greet. Refrain from a clenched-teeth smile.

Pay attention to your body language. Breathe deeply and slowly and relax. Keep your shoulders back and your hands quiet. No hair spinning around your pinky, lip chewing, squinting your eyes, or overblinking.

Raise technical issues, if necessary. If something goes south—say, your internet connection blips or your interviewer's does, or you're having trouble with your computer's camera or microphone—speak up. If it happens during a recorded interview, just abort and contact the recruiter to explain and reschedule.

Say thanks. End your interview by saying, "Thank you for considering me for the job. I look forward to hearing from you." Smile, and continue eyeing the camera until the interview disconnects.

Being a Star in Automated Interviews

Automated interviews are those in which a recorded interviewer asks questions, and you're given a set amount of time to record each answer.

Many candidates, especially older candidates, who tend to be more familiar with interacting with human beings than with performing in front of a webcam, may have a rough time with automated interviews. Creating rapport with an interviewer who is just a taped video image when you have to answer in two minutes or less can be quite a challenge.

It really is more like acting than interviewing, so practice. Sit yourself in front of your computer screen camera, set it up to record, and rehearse answering questions until you're at ease with the format. Watch and critique your recorded responses to improve your delivery. All the suggestions in the previous section for video interviews come into play here as well.

C H A P T E R

Military Spouses and Remote Jobs

As I pored over all the job listings for remote jobs on the FlexJobs website, I was amazed by the number of companies that have a special endorsement: "The U.S. Department of Defense recognizes this employer as a Military Spouse Employment Partner (MSEP)."

It's really hard for many military spouses to hang on-to jobs when partners are redeployed to new duties every few years. Finding a job that you can take with you can make a huge difference in your work-life balance and your family's financial well-being.

As I discovered, the FlexJobs database, for instance, which is updated daily with verified flexible roles, has great options for military spouses. FlexJobs has partnered with the Department of Defense as an official Military Spouse Employment Partner, which means they've committed to recruiting and hiring military spouses. The company also joined the U.S. Chamber of Commerce Foundation's Hiring our Heroes campaign, which highlights the numerous issues military spouses face, such as frequent relocation.

Here are ten remote jobs that the crackerjack team at Flexjobs.com and Remote.co tells me are popular with military spouses. For more details on these jobs, see Chapter 1.

Account Manager. A remote account manager creates solid relationships with customers, onramps new clients, communicates project updates to internal and external stakeholders, and guarantees the timely and effective delivery of projects.

Customer Service Representative. Customer service reps can wear a lot of hats, depending on the employer. You might answer customer questions, sell products or services, solve problems for customers, and manage payment processing.

Marketing Strategist. Marketing strategists might create and apply strategic plans, conduct research, monitor marketing plan performance, oversee analytics, and more.

Project Manager. Project managers turn concepts into deliverables, outline project scope, keep projects on schedule, act as a link between teams, and manage vendors and other partners. Project managers in demand often have exact experience in certain career areas, say, IT, advertising, or software development.

Recruiter. Recruiters are the ones trolling for new candidates for jobs employers are trying to fill; they interview candidates and help them get launched as employees.

Technical Writer. Duties often embrace writing technical documents such as user manuals, product specifications, and more. Expertise in specific topics is typically required.

Transcriber. Transcribers do just what it sounds like. You turn the spoken word in audio files into written transcripts. You must have excellent spelling, listening, and grammar skills. A fast typing speed is often required. Transcribing from one language to another is often a marketable skill.

Travel Specialist. The bottom line of these positions is often smooth customer service to help clients plan trips, book transportation, and make hotel reservations.

Tutor. A tutor provides academic online virtual help and teaching to students of all ages and levels of education. A bachelor's degree and subject matter expertise are usually required.

Web Designer. Common duties include writing HTML/CSS code, designing web page layouts, producing advertising banners for web sites, applying new features, and more.

What Is the Military Spouse Employment Partnership?

The Military Spouse Employment Partnership is an initiative of the Department of Defense's Spouse Education and Career Opportunities (SECO) program with the objective of helping military spouses find jobs and portable careers.

The partnership includes more than 390 partners or military-friendly employers. For more information, visit the MSEP Job Search on MySECO (myseco.militaryonesource.mil/portal/).

The site has thousands of job postings from its hundreds of partner employers seeking "qualified military spouse applicants." With the MSEP Job Search, you can do the following:

- View Hot Jobs—job opportunities that need to be filled immediately—located across the United States and around the world.
- Search for jobs using job titles, keywords, and locations.
- Refine your search by selecting industry, partner, job type, and location radius.
- You can research organizations on the site with links to the organization's websites and social media platforms. And set up your own account and profile with contact information, work experience, education, and job search location.

The search engine also allows you to opt-in to allow recruiters vetted by MSEP to contact you.

And the MySECO Resume Toolkit will help create your résumé. There are sample résumés and cover letters to give you some ideas. You can create and store multiple résumés.

For assistance with applying for a job, planning for an interview, and honing your résumé, you can also call Military OneSource at 800-342-9647 to speak with a SECO career coach. You can also visit the Employment Readiness and Career Connections lifecycle stages of MySECO for tips, cover letter suggestions, networking assistance, mentoring connections, and more. For additional guidance, use the Live Chat feature on the MySECO website.

Veterans challenged with finding employment due to injury, disability, or simply adjusting to corporate culture are also increasingly seeking remote work. "Soft skills" such as flexibility, adaptability, and loyalty are critical skills that veterans can bring to organizations.

Remote work offers opportunities to veterans with unique challenges segueing back into civilian life, such as injury, disability, or purely adapting to corporate culture. And when you think about it, there's no better job-seeker demographic if you're looking for someone who knows how to be a team player.

Google and Military Spouse Jobs

A search feature on Google allows you to type your field of work and "work from home" or a similar phrase into the Google engine search box and specifically pull out jobs that can be done remotely. In truth, it can help anyone, but when it launched it was touted as being aimed at military spouses.

Google also has a scholarship partnership with Syracuse University's Institute for Veterans and Military Families, Onward to Opportunity (ivmf.syracuse.edu/programs/career-training) that gives scholarships for the Google IT Professional Support Certificate program (grow.google/programs/it-support). Some of these programs are earmarked specifically for military spouses. The company also partnered with Blue Star Families to teach digital skills to military spouse remote employees.

Work-from-Home Companies That Offer Jobs for Veterans and Military Spouses

One website that I encourage all of you to check out is Job-Hunt.Org (job-hunt.org). It is absolutely one of the best sites I know for great career advice with articles and so much more.

Job-Hunt's Job Search Expert for Veterans, Diane Hudson, is a military transition job-search strategist and career coach, whom I have tapped for expert advice over the years for my columns. She designs and composes military conversion résumés and helps position service members for employment in corporate or federal America. Diane holds eight industry credentials, including Certified Leadership and Talent Management Coach and Federal Job Search Trainer and Counselor, and owns Career Marketing Techniques.

Here is her short list of top military-friendly companies:
Union Pacific Railroad
Home Depot

J.B. Hunt Transport Services, Inc.
TriWest Healthcare Alliance
Northrop Grumman Corporation
Sodexo, Inc.
Schneider National
Sears Holdings Corporation
Bank of America
State Farm Insurance Exelon Corporation Financial Services
DynCorp International
Corrections Corporation of America
U-Haul
Brink's U.S.
American Eurocopter
BAE Systems, Inc
Capital One: Work-from-home opportunities at Capital One include customer service positions, analysis, and data science roles.
CarMax
Comcast
National Security Agency (NSA)
PNC Bank
PricewaterhouseCoopers
Sysco Corporation
Wegmans

Other military spouse-friendly companies that have popped up in my reporting include:

Amazon: Amazon focuses on providing flexible opportunities for military spouses to work from home, so they can keep their job even if they're faced with frequent relocations. Many of the work-from-home jobs are customer-service based, yet there are also work-from-home opportunities in project management, software development, and recruiting.

Convergys: Convergys offers work-from-home positions in the healthcare industry, customer service, and sales. They also offer training and opportunities for growth.

Dell: Computer technology company Dell provides military spouses with jobs that can be done anywhere their spouse is deployed. Many of these telecommuting jobs are in marketing, customer service, and support.

Enterprise Holdings: Enterprise Holdings is a rental car company providing work-at-home jobs mainly focused in their customer service division, assisting customers with their rentals and helping them with any concerns.

Humana: The insurance company Humana lists many work-from-home opportunities in customer service, care coordination, and client sales. They also list jobs available for bilingual employees and those with medical backgrounds.

JPMorgan Chase & Co.: Global financial services company JPMorgan Chase & Co. offers work-from-home positions for those experienced in the banking industry, including mid-level roles.

Progressive: Insurance company Progressive mostly offers customer service positions for work-from-home flexibility, full-time hours, and competitive pay.

SYKES is a digital marketing and customer service outsourcing company and through their Home Jobs division, they offer many telecommuting roles to military spouses.

Travelers: Travelers recruits and hires military spouses during their quarterly hiring event MOJO (Military Officers Job Opportunities). Work-from-home and telecommuting positions are listed on FlexJobs and include a wide-range of opportunities such as underwriter, customer service, training consultant, and auditor.

U-Haul: Remote jobs at moving company U-Haul include customer service positions in sales and reservations. These positions provide flexibility, competitive pay, and training.

USAA: USAA serves military members and their families with insurance, credit, and banking services. Because of their close work with the military, they're a premier military employer as well. Telecommuting positions are available in fraud prevention, analysis, customer service, appraisals, and many other areas. Many of the positions do require employees to live within traveling distance of a corporate office (AZ, CO, FL, MD, NY, or TX), but they offer flexibility and accommodations for the unique needs of military spouses.

Verizon: Verizon has a Military Spouse Talent Network and actively recruits for open positions. These customer service and support positions provide training, competitive salary, and flexible shifts.

Xerox: Through the Heroes@Home program, Xerox provides veterans and their spouses with home employment opportunities. They actively recruit veterans and their spouses. The work-from-home jobs include customer service, help desk, system development, and leadership roles.

A Training Resource for Military Spouses and Veterans

Career Step. Career Step (careerstep.com) helps active duty military members, veterans, and their spouses receive job training to launch them into a new career. Classes and certifications are available online, so it's easy to do the work on your own schedule from wherever you're located.

Programs offered include medical billing and coding, veterinary assisting, medical transcription, and many other fields. Career Step also provides students with funding options, financial aid, and military discounts. You can find out more about the MYCAA military spouse education at their website (careerstep.com/military or careerstep.com/military#military-spouses).

Target Work Easily Handled at Home

Another columnist on the Job-Hunt.org site is a valued colleague of mine, Nancy Collamer, author of *Second-Act Careers: 50+ Ways to Profit from Your Passions During Semi-Retirement.* Her website is MyLifestyleCareer.com. Here is her advice for finding a work-from-home job that she wrote for the Job-Hunt.org site. It applies to all remote work seekers, but I thought it fit nicely into this military spouse section.

In general, these are jobs that can be completed independently, using basic home-based office equipment (personal computer and a telephone).

Examples of these jobs include:

- Accounting tasks (e.g., bookkeeping, loan processing, mortgage processing)
- Clerical duties (e.g., data entry, transcription, word processing)
- Computer programming
- Desktop publishing.
- Customer service
- Internet-related tasks (e.g., research, web design, writing copy)
- Market research/telemarketing

- Recruiting
- Sales
- Writing, proofreading, and copyediting

Certain industries tend to hire more telecommuters than others. Companies that have a large need for telephone-based customer service jobs (think airlines, insurance, and software firms) can be decent places to look for home-based employment.

Other examples of telecommuting-friendly settings include banks that hire home-based mortgage brokers, home inspection companies that hire licensed inspectors, and executive recruiting firms that hire home-based research assistants.

There are also a handful of companies that recruit customer care agents who work out of their homes as contract employees.

TOP WORK-FROM-HOME JOB POSITIONS

As I reviewed in Part 1, here are most common work-from-home titles found on Flexjobs.com and ones that military spouses might consider:

- Accountant
- Engineer
- Teacher/faculty/tutor/instructor
- Writer
- Consultant
- Program manager
- Project manager
- Customer service representative
- Business development manager
- Account manager/account executive
- Recruiter
- Sales representative
- Web developer
- Medical coder
- Territory sales manager
- Nurse
- Data analyst
- Editor
- Case manager
- UX/UI designer

C H A P T E R

Job Hunting Advice from Steve

P eople looking for remote jobs often tell me they find the process frustrating. They apply for posted jobs and never hear back—the "black hole" syndrome. Steve Dalton, program director for daytime career services at Duke University's Fuqua School of Business and author of *The 2-Hour Job Search: Using Technology to Get the Right Job Faster,* sympathizes, but he also has important advice: You need to know how to look for work in this age of virtual job search.

"Sadly, every year I see dozens of very smart people voluntarily subject themselves to situations with high competition and low odds of success (online job postings, most commonly)," Dalton writes. "Submitting résumés online lets job seekers feel like they're looking for a job, but it's like watching someone beating up a vending machine completely unwilling to accept that it just ate his or her money."

The Two-Hour Job Search

After reading *The 2-Hour Job Search,* I interviewed Dalton for my column on NextAvenue.org to hear more; below you'll see my eight favorite tips he offered.

Now about that "two-hour" notion: In reality, the two hours are not how long it will actually take you to get hired, but the time it will take to winnow down your list of forty potential employers and find networking connections who can be your insider booster or advocate. That's a person who can bring your résumé to the right person, make an introduction, and help you get an interview.

"In practice, you start with forty employers that you rank in terms of priority, but no job seeker I have worked with who has followed the two-hour search has ever gotten past fifteen without getting hired," Dalton says.

The Power of Boosters for a Job Hunt

Boosters are the people who love their current job and take an interest in helping others advance their careers, according to Dalton. "It essentially boils down to purposeful relationship building," he says. "Even if you are not the perfect fit for the job, but you can get someone to advocate for you, you can jump ahead of people who might have that fit, but don't have a champion."

Dalton's people-centric approach hits me as particularly wise considering that not all that long ago the Federal Trade Commission (FTC) charged two companies with bilking people of hundreds of thousands of dollars annually for sham job placement and résumé repair services. To get an interview, job seekers had to pay upfront fees of $1,200 to $2,500. In many instances, the defendants pocketed consumers' money knowing the job opportunities were fake, according to the FTC. A federal court halted the scheme and froze the defendants' assets at the FTC's request.

8 Tips for a Job Hunt

Now, as promised, here are my eight favorite job-seeking tips from Dalton. They can be summarized in three words: people, skills, and patience:

1. **Don't be embarrassed.** "There's a lot of needless embarrassment and shame associated with job searching, especially mid- or late-career, when nobody at that age has been rigorously taught how to job search, particularly in the online job posting era.

Don't be ashamed. Embrace this as a new skill set—turning strangers into advocates on demand," says Dalton.

2. **Get contacts at your prospective employers to talk about why they are so good at their work.** "Set up an informational interview. This can take some persistence. Find people whose work you admire, preferably at companies where you want to work, and reach out by phone or in person to learn about their jobs," says Dalton.

3. **During these conversations, resist the temptation to sell yourself.** "It is the sell-yourself mentality that sends the conversations off the rails. Focus on really learning. When you embrace the humbling process of no longer selling yourself and instead dedicate yourself to listening, you will get so far, so quickly," says Dalton.

4. **Hone your listening skills.** "When I give my talks, I show the audience a GIF of a dog cuddling up to its owner because dogs are experts at this. When they look at their owner, there is not another person in that dog's world. They block everyone out. They are singularly focused. We don't love dogs because they are good conversationalists. We love them because we are the only person in their world when they look at us. That is the key to listening well," says Dalton.

5. **Be likeable.** "The point is not to tell them why you are so great. The point is to let them know that they have been heard. That you are open to learning and are passionate about learning about their employer or the work they do. You are perceived to be likeable if you are listening. It's how you build a booster relationship. It is a counterintuitive concept," says Dalton.

6. **Take advantage of LinkedIn.** "I don't endorse a lot of career-related websites, but I do consider LinkedIn a must. Even better, it's free [if you don't sign up for the premium version]. A LinkedIn People Search helps find contacts at a target employer. It's six degrees of separation. You supply the name of an employer and it shows the closest connection you have to someone who works there. If it's someone who shares an alumni connection with you, even better. LinkedIn Groups are also helpful to find connections, or people to reach out to with a short email (fewer than one hundred words) that has no mention of a job, just your connection to him or her and expressing an interest in learning about a topic," says Dalton.

7. **Use job boards for research.** "Online job postings aren't good for getting you a job, but they're great information about what sorts of jobs are available in a particular city. I recommend using Indeed for meta-information. what employers are looking for in your city, even different jobs than what you're looking for. I always figure the specific jobs listed are already spoken for. The chance of a random applicant online going through and getting that job is a longshot. Remember, you are looking for people. I have never heard of a job seeker finding a job online who didn't have a booster," says Dalton.

8. **Don't fear technology.** "The good news is there is really no intimidating technology anyone has to learn to pull this off. Use a simple spreadsheet to create your list of employers and LinkedIn and Google searches to learn about trends in the industry that interests you and to discover smaller companies in the field doing interesting things that you may not have known. You may also tap into databases such as an alumni one or Dun & Bradstreet's Hoovers to learn about competitors of companies you're interested in that may tip you off to less obvious employers. Back in the old days it was accidental networking; you meet or know somebody who knows somebody. Now the game is about having those accidental meetings, but on purpose. That is terrifying, but not a lot of new technology to learn," says Dalton.

Making It Work

A Cigna survey, Loneliness and the Workplace 2020 U.S. Report, surveyed 10,441 adults online to measure loneliness in America, and especially in the workplace. To measure loneliness, the researchers asked people questions using the UCLA Loneliness Scale; a score of 43 or higher out of 80 is considered lonely.

Among the study's findings: Remote workers are more likely to feel lonely than people working in offices with colleagues nearby. More than half of remote workers surveyed (53 percent) said they always or sometimes feel isolated from others, quite a bit higher than the 48 percent of people who work "in-person." Similarly, 53 percent of remote workers said they feel they lack companionship always or sometimes while only 46 percent of non-remote workers do.

Without adequate social interaction, loneliness can create depression and a range of other emotional and physical health com-plications.

Yes, home-based employment can get lonely, but doesn't have to, in my opinion, and I've been at it for years.

As I wrote in my introduction to this book, I've never before talked to so many workers who quickly adapted during the coronavi-rus work from home orders to using communication technology like

Zoom conferencing and are embracing it. Virtual meetups with friends, family, and co-workers became a breeze and a stress buster in short order when the stay-at-home orders kicked in.

That said, I do envision that in the aftermath of the pandemic that ran through our country, we will all emerge from our homes eager to connect with others. It's hard to speculate on what the new rules of social interactions will be moving forward. In some fashion, use the advice below to help you formulate the best way for you to find ways for the human touch. There is no replacement for it.

Three Easy Ways to Combat the Isolation

1. **Make that date.** Take time for a break, pause, push back from your workspace. We all benefit to some degree from face-to-face connections. Plan time to meet friends, other remote workers you know who live nearby, or office-bound co-workers once a week, if you can. This can be a coffee, lunch, or even an after-work meet-and-greet. But make yourself get out of the house and connect with someone.

   As I have discussed, setting workplace boundaries is essential to making remote work a success for you and your employer. "The secret to setting boundaries is to intentionally and purposefully incorporate meetings, breaks, vacations, calls, coffee with friends, and activities into your calendar," says Dan Schawbel, managing partner of Workplace Intelligence. "By doing this, it will force good behavior and alleviate your burnout. Remember that burnout is *counter*productive. You may think you are getting more done, but it's at the cost of your health and happiness, which will eventually wear you down and cause you to quit," he says.

   I personally have a really hard time with this. Taking time to meet someone in person is a time suck, especially when you have deadlines looming, and who doesn't? That said, I've found a lovely local coffee shop around the corner from my house to have meet and greets.

   I like to give the owners the business, and it's an easy place for most people to get to if they live in Washington, D.C., or are visiting from out of town. It's located close to the Metro.

Without question, the day of the coffee or lunch, I complain and am annoyed that I agreed to the get-together. What was I thinking? I have this and this and this to do. It breaks my work rhythm. And I have to get dressed in something other than my leggings or jeans and put on some makeup, and that can take time, too.

Afterward, however—and I'm not making this up—I'm genuinely buzzing with energy and wonder why I don't do this more often. I'm recharged. I've made a new connection, caught up with a dear friend in town, and so on. It's a boost psychologically. And if I'm meeting someone who needs friendly job-hunting advice, tips for launching their dream business, or mentoring, I feel even better from being able to give back in some fashion and to encourage their efforts.

So do it, do it, do it. It is time well spent. You don't have to make it open-ended. Set a specific time for the break.

Another option if you are "owned by a dog," as I am, you might schedule a dog walking date a few times a week with someone in your neighborhood who also has this activity on their daily regime. Take half an hour at least, stretch your legs, and your furry friend's legs, too, soak in some fresh air, and refresh your eyes from staring at the computer screen. Engage with another person on something other than your work. Bingo. Smile.

2. **Attend events.** I also make a point of going to events that relate to my work or my alma mater. I don't do this more than once a month, but it's a networking opportunity, and I usually learn something. Sign up for a lecture series. Take a class at community college or a local library from time to time.

3. **Set up your "office" in a new spot.** Changing your "work-space" scenery can give you a boost. Remote work doesn't always mean you have to work from home. You might opt to work in a co-working hub, or a coffee shop, an independent bookstore with a café, or a community library one or two days a week. Fact: I have been known to set up my laptop in the barn tack room where I stable my horse. There's a strong Wi-Fi connection, and that soothing aroma of leather and horses.

FIVE TOP LOCATIONS TO BE A DIGITAL NOMAD

As I have been telling you, in an increasingly digital world, the old concept of a physical office is quickly fading away.

A survey by PwC, an accounting and consulting firm, found that for Millennials, work is a *thing,* not a *place.*

For many remote workers, the "office" lives chiefly on the cloud, accessible from anyplace that has Wi-Fi—making any place in the world a potential office.

The experts at International Living (Internationalliving.com) identified five good-value locales around the world where the infrastructure is solid, the sun sparkles, and digital nomads can create a low-cost home base.

Among the digital nomad ranks are a whole range of professions, including software developers, graphic designers, copywriters, and consultants—both working remotely for their employers and freelancing.

To help narrow in on a destination and provide a sample of what the untethered life is all about, *International Living* compiled a list of the top five destination recommendations for digital nomads. Here's their review:

Medellín, Colombia

Nicknamed "The City of Eternal Spring," Medellín sits at 5,000 feet above sea level and offers flawless springlike weather year-round. With daytime highs in the mid-70s to low-80s°F and very little humidity, the city makes it very easy to live and work comfortably.

Over the past few decades, Medellín has shaken off the shadow of its dark past to become one of the most progressive cities in the world, winning awards for innovation and design, and earning the moniker "Medellín Miracle" for its impressive social transformation. As such, it has attracted digital nomads in droves in search of up-and-coming, low-cost destinations, and now has a well-established remote-working infrastructure.

During the past five years, the number of co-working spaces in Medellín has grown exponentially to include everything from well-organized formal settings with a corporate, interactive vibe to quiet, small, intimate spaces to "hot desks" (unassigned desk space in an open plan office).

The exchange rate in Colombia has been hovering around 3,000 pesos to the U.S. dollar for about the past three years. This makes an already low cost of living even lower. It is possible to live on $1,500 to $2,000 per month in many parts of Medellín.

Lisbon, Portugal

Lisbon was always a top candidate for the most popular city in Europe for digital nomads. It is one of the cheapest capital cities in Western Europe; it has 300 days of sunshine per year; the winters are mild; the nightlife, coffee, and food scene can compete with anywhere in the world; there is access to beaches; great healthcare; and the powerful allure of yellow trams, azulejos tiles, terracotta rooftops, and custard tarts make it irresistible.

But what makes Lisbon exceptional is how well it has adjusted to the influx of digital nomads. It has a reputation as one of the most welcoming digital-nomad scenes in the world. There are digital-nomad meetups held every week, with active Facebook groups and events run by digital-nomad accommodation startups like NomadX.

Portugal has invested a lot in its Wi-Fi infrastructure, with 90 percent coverage nationwide and an average internet speed of 21 mbps in Lisbon. There is free Wi-Fi in many of Lisbon's parks and cafés, and most Airbnbs will come equipped. A landline internet connection costs $20 to $30 a month, depending on speed.

Rent in Lisbon runs about $600 a month and up. However, shorter-term solutions such as Airbnb offer one-bedroom apartments in the city for $55 a night off-season, and $90 a night at the height of summer.

Chiang Mai, Thailand

Chiang Mai has long been considered the spiritual home of digital nomads, and is highly recommended for anyone starting out on their remote-working journey.

What makes Chiang Mai such an easy starting point is that, well before it became a popular digital nomad destination, it was a popular retirement haven for expats from around the world. This means that there is an established Westernized community within the fabric of the city, with plenty of cafés, restaurants, social groups, and entertainment networks for every taste—dwarfing the size of most metropolitan digital-nomad communities many times over.

Aside from being low cost, with pleasant temperatures, Chiang Mai offers a more romantic reason for its popularity, too. The ancient city, filled with temples and historic treasures, melds comfortably with the sprawling modern metropolis that has built up around it. It has a laidback atmosphere, and it feels more like a sleepy country town than a chaotic city.

Not only can digital nomads save thousands per month while living in Chiang Mai, but they will compromise on nothing in terms of lifestyle experiences.

Mexico City, Mexico

Mexico City shares a similar story to Medellín, in that it has entirely regenerated as a city in recent years, becoming one of the most powerful cultural and economic hubs in Latin American.

At over 573 square miles, the city feels massive, but most expats and digital nomads—as well as the capital's 1,200-plus startups—tend to congregate in just a few central districts.

Colonias Juarez, Condesa, Roma, San Rafael, St. Maria de Ribera, and Polanco are all within walking distance from the city's incredible museums, parks, and monuments. Nightlife is electric, from dance clubs to underground jazz bars and salsa dives. But also within these buzzing districts, startup activity is attracting many local meetups, big-name conferences, recognized accelerators, and a community of co-working spaces.

Internet speed here is excellent and available in most coffee shops and businesses. Even though there is no free citywide system, Wi-Fi is available in many of the central parks and several lines of the metro.

The city is also extremely affordable. In Colonias, Roma, and Condesa, average rent is $500 to $900 a month. Airbnb has meant lots of great spaces have opened up that allow temporary residents to really dig into neighborhoods and the city.

Food in restaurants, on the street, and in the markets is relatively inexpensive and you can find products and cuisines from across the country and around the world. A remote worker can easily live in Mexico City on $2,000 a month and that includes everything: rent, food, utilities, and transportation.

Tallinn, Estonia

Given their flexibility, digital nomads tend to wander—which provides them an opportunity to follow their travel whim (or the sun).

That's useful, because Tallinn, Estonia, is not a year-round destination. Winter temperatures can fall as low as −20°F, with heavy snow. Summers are milder, reaching the mid-70s°F. But what it lacks in climate, it makes up for elsewhere.

What Tallinn offers above all else is a glimpse of the future for digital nomads. In Estonia, internet access is enshrined as a human right and everything happens online. With the second-fastest public Wi-Fi in the world (next only to its Eastern European neighbor, Lithuania), citizens can vote, secure mortgages, open bank accounts, and even open businesses in minutes, without ever leaving their café table.

Recently, Estonia announced the first official visa for digital nomads. The permit will entitle nomads to 365 days of working in Estonia, including 90 days' travel in the Schengen area. They have also created an e-residency program, making it possible to start an EU-based company online.

Estonia is creating the framework for the new digital nomad world, and Tallinn is at the heart of it. The city has approximately 500,000 people, but despite its size, Tallinn actually feels small and quiet. The streets aren't jammed with traffic, calm green parks are everywhere, and even in one of the busiest intersections, at the crossroads of old town and the modern tech town, Hobujaama, you never feel like you're in a large city. Tallinn is very pedestrian-friendly. There are countless tree-lined paths and forest walkways throughout the city.

Restaurant food is typically $8 to $15 per meal. A comfortable and modern Airbnb on the edge of town is $800 for the month. An Uber costs just $3 to $6 for a ride into downtown. The city bus system is also affordable, at $30 for the month. Coworking spaces dot the city, with hot desks available from about $6 per day or $106 per month.

Twelve Tips to Work from Home Successfully

Own It

Working from home requires discipline, whether that is ignoring distractions during the day or setting your work hours for when you're most productive.

You also have to determine how dependent you are on other people when you're at work. Working from home can be lonely, and increased isolation can even lead to sapped productivity and motivation. It also requires some unpredictable skills, such as the ability to troubleshoot your own IT problems.

Generally speaking, a successful remote worker is somebody who's going to be very comfortable in their own skin and able to have that focus and have the discipline.

And as I wrote earlier, some employers may say they support remote workers, but in reality maybe your manager isn't happy about giving you autonomy over where and when you work. They may equate remote work with less work. With the right discipline from you, it's really all about working hard and having a life.

Have a Specific Place Exclusively for Work for Productivity *and* for Tax Benefits

It's important to designate a space where you can set your own boundaries. This also means telling your friends and family not to infringe on that location. It's amazing how many people think you're not really working. They call you; they stop by. You have to approach it just like you do if you're going to work.

Not only can an at-home office potentially help your productivity, it can also save you money on your taxes, especially for those who may be self-employed and have to shell out expenses for both Social Security and Medicare taxes.

But you must file Form 8829, "Expenses for Business Use of Your Home." You can read all the home-office rules in IRS Publication 587.

My advice: In general, to write off home-office outlays, you must use the "area" for work only and on a regular or constant basis, either as your primary place of business or as a setting to meet with clients or to do paperwork such as writing invoices, ordering supplies, and making phone calls. I suggest you snap a pic of the space, too, so you have a record in case the IRS is ever curious.

If you're a full-time employee at a business, you will only qualify for the deductions if the company doesn't provide you with an office within their workplace. (See the list below of freelancer deductions that may apply to you.)

Make Time for Face-Time

Just because you work alone at home doesn't mean you can't network, as I said earlier. To avoid feeling like you're out of the loop, commute to your employer's local office from time to time to connect with your co-workers. That might mean inviting teammates to lunch or asking for a meeting with your managers.

Don't worry if your employer doesn't have a local office. Try to find other employees working remotely in your area, maybe even those who work at the same company, and invite them to happy hour or coffee. Attend conferences and events in your area if you don't have local co-workers.

Ask Your Manager to Evaluate Your Performance

What are the expectations of me? How will my performance be measured to ensure productivity? These are the two big questions you need to have answered for before you start your job. And you must always keep these issues on the front-burner. Not doing this could cost you.

If you're not working at the office, you can often be out of sight, out of mind for a promotion, or you could miss out on the opportunity to do a cool project. There are lots of ways that you're not top of mind for a manager to pull you in on something. To truly love and be engaged in your job, you want to be able to raise your hand and ask for new duties and new prospects.

When you work from home, you have to communicate more than ever. That includes asking for feedback from your manager as if you were an employee at the office. When you communicate with your manager and discuss your at-home work performance, you're ensuring that they feel they're getting what they need from you, and you're getting the feedback you need from them.

Make Sure You Have Enough Insurance

It's probably a good idea to get an insurance rider in case the FedEx man trips. If you file a homeowner's (or renter's) claim for losses that stemmed from an undisclosed home office, your insurer may not cover it. If you have valuable equipment, you might want to protect it from theft or damage as well.

My advice: The least expensive way to add insurance is to tack on a rider to your existing homeowner's or renter's insurance policy. The cost might be around $100 a year for around $2,500 of additional coverage. For more, consult the Insurance Information Institute (www.iii.org) in New York City, an industry trade group and information clearinghouse.

Declutter Your Office

When people feel low on energy, often it's because they're not clearing out as they go. Their inbox is overflowing. Their desk is a disaster. Their file drawers are jammed.

Decluttering is liberating and empowering. You are saying, "This is valuable; this is not." It's a physical, practical way to engage in making decisions about your life and what you want to do with it. Getting rid of stuff brings a new perspective.

Home-office clutter can take a toll on your productivity. You might make it a practice to scan receipts and documents, then shred or recycle them.

Set up an organized filing system. And spend the money to have a great chair that doesn't hurt your back. Arrange furniture so you're not at risk for falling over wires or cords. I make a point of straightening my desk up at the end of every day. Simple habits.

Find a Positive Image to Inspire You

I call mine "going to my happy place." I close my eyes and visualize a green field in the Virginia countryside with a sweeping view of the Blue Ridge Mountains. I go there in my head and sit. It calms me down. I feel peaceful and my attitude shifts.

If you want a more concrete focal point, tape a picture of a special image on your office wall, away from your computer and phone. That way, you'll have to turn to look directly at it, which can be transporting. The very action of directing your attention away from your work opens up the door in your day for a respite, a restart, and a new view. It's reviving and centering at the same time.

Pay Attention to Your Eyes

Avoid eyestrain by placing your desktop or laptop monitor just above eye level and an arm's length away. And supplement any natural light in your home office without reducing the contrast on your computer screen.

Set up Your Computer and Desk to Prevent Repetitive-Motion Injuries

Things like good lighting and comfort are not to be ignored when you're spending hours in front of your computer.

Keep your keyboard and mouse level with where your elbows are when you're seated, as I mention above. Sometimes I sit on a couch and stretch out, but I always place a pillow beneath my laptop to bring it to the right level. I also place a rolled towel or pillow in the small of my back to keep me from hunching over.

A healthy and productive remote work setup is essential. Ergonomics matters. From picking the right monitor, laptop, and noise-cancelling headphones, to your chair and even a laptop stand can make a huge difference to your productivity, your physical health, and your mental well-being.

To save on some psychological frustration, make sure your Wi-Fi connection is as robust as you can: Shift your router or move your workstation near to get an enhanced connection.

Listen to your body. I've talked to many work-from-homers who complain of terrible neck pain or aching backs. Are you, like me, guilty of sitting on your sofa, hunched over your laptop, working for hours lost in the vacuum of time? That's a recipe for long-term physical ailments such as carpal tunnel syndrome, muscle strains, and lower back injuries.

There are simple solutions to help prevent this, among them ergonomic desk accessories and office furniture. I've found that, in many ways, it often comes down to good posture. (I taped a note to my mouse to remind me. It simply says: Shoulders!)

One easy fix is elevating your computer screen to prevent you from hunching over, as I do with my makeshift pillow, but there are better ways, so I would advise asking around or checking with your employer or even an office supply store manager to see what they recommend. A laptop stand, for example, with a remote keyboard and mouse, can help keep your arms in a 90-degree position while you type and can help combat the strain on your wrists.

CYBERSECURITY: BETTER SAFE THAN SORRY

There can be a downside to working from home when it comes to cybersecurity. Most employers will have support and guide you through setting up your computer and connections, but a few basics to keep in mind:

Refrain from clicking on an email that looks suspicious. Carefully look at the email of the sender before opening. This is a tough one to suss out, but pause before you open it.

Stay on top of your passwords. Make sure all your email accounts, applications, and various devices from cellphones to laptops are password protected and change them periodically. The most secure passwords have at least eight characters, but my advice is to use the longest one that you're permitted to on the system. Use a variety of passwords and always avoid personal information. And yes, make sure you have a way to keep track of them.

Keep your software programs up-to-date. Apple, Google, Microsoft, and other players regularly update the version of the software you are running on your devices, so take advantage of those "update now" prompts.

Make sure your devices have encryption. Your employer will probably require encryption on your devices to protect client information. But even if they do, you should add it, if possible. Typically, email applications that are free don't have this protection. Premium versions generally have the encryption available by default.

The hard disk on your computer is probably protected by default. Check under Settings and System to find out. Mac computers, for example, have an app called Filevault. If you don't have it, you can probably upgrade on the Windows operating system.

> **Do your best to secure your home Wi-Fi.** Check your settings to be certain that your Wi-Fi is private and password protected.
> **Run regular backups.** My computer reminds me frequently how many days it has been since I've backed it up, which is great. I have had my computer go belly-up and lost everything from the previous two months because I ignored it!
> Online backup services are offered by Microsoft OneDrive, Google Drive, and Apple iCloud as well as independent providers like Carbonite. I also back up important files on an external hard drive that I connect to my laptop with a USB cable. Once connected, you select individual files or folders to copy onto the external hard drive.
> **Add an antivirus or malware security product.** These programs offer an extra level of security to defend you against malware and block hackers. You can find product reviews in publications such as *PC* magazine. Some of the top ones include Norton 360 Deluxe, Malwarebytes Free, and Webroot SecureAnywhere AntiVirus.

Don't Neglect Your Retirement Savings

Freelancers without an employer retirement plan can set savings aside in a traditional IRA (Independent Retirement Arrangement), a Roth IRA, a simplified employee pension (SEP-IRA), or a solo 401(k). For more details, go to the IRS website (irs.gov/retirement-plans/individual-retirement-arrangements-iras).

With a traditional IRA, your contributions may be deductible if you aren't covered by another employer plan, and the growth is tax-deferred. But if you have a spouse covered by a plan, income limits may apply; for more details, check the IRS website.

With a Roth IRA, your contributions are not tax-deductible, but your money grows tax-free, and you'll pay no taxes on your distributions as long as you follow the withdrawal rules. (Normally, you must have held the account for five years and be 59½ or older.) There are income limits for Roth IRAs.

A simplified employee pension or SEP-IRA is a tax-deductible retirement plan that's appealing if you're a single employee. You can typically contribute up to 25 percent of your compensation.

A one-participant or solo 401(k) is a retirement plan for self-employed people without employees (a spouse is an exception). You can usually sock away pretax, up to 25 percent of your pay, with a cut-off contribution limit that fluctuates annually.

These retirement accounts are offered at most mutual fund companies and brokerage firms. They're easy to set up online: enter your bank information, how often you want to invest, and the amount you want to transfer.

When it comes to hassle-free tax and retirement planning for self-employed workers, repeat this mantra: automate, automate, automate.

Pay Attention to Taxes

If you work as a contractor, and not as a full-time employee, you are probably responsible for shepherding your taxes without someone parsing them out paycheck by paycheck.

I always balk when it's quarterly tax time again. I know that dreaded feeling. Still, send in that check to avoid a possible penalty from the IRS for underpayment of taxes. Independent contractors who are paid only for work performed, in general, must pay federal taxes and FICA on their income. You will probably need to pay estimated taxes throughout the year instead of once a year on April 15.

My advice: Go to the IRS Self-Employed Individual Tax Center (irs.gov) to help you understand how to pay federal taxes as an independent contractor. Depending on the location of your home office, you may be required to file state and local income and business taxes as well.

Diligent recording of business expenses is essential. The easiest way to differentiate personal from work expenses is to use a designated bank account and credit card for your work-related outlays.

Fluctuations in pay make it tricky to set aside the correct amount for yearly tax bills. And work-from-home job opportunities often fall under the contractor or self-employed category, so an employer may not withhold taxes for you, or allow you to qualify to participate in an employer-sponsored retirement plan.

The process can be a scramble. It's not uncommon for self-employed workers to have to write big checks in April to cover federal and state income taxes. Then they have to write another one to fund their retirement plans.

The chief reason for the sticker shock: Freelance pay can fluctuate from year to year, so it can be difficult to estimate your annual total income in advance. One year you might work a seasonal job, for instance, and the next year tackle a series of part-time or contract assignments. Those fluctuations make setting aside the correct amount for your yearly tax bills tricky. Meanwhile, how much income you collect also directly affects the sum you can set aside in many retirement accounts.

According to a recent T. Rowe Price study, 26 percent of Boomers and 32 percent of Gen X respondents work independently in some capacity.

Based on your previous year's federal tax return, you (or your accountant) must figure out the total amount you will owe Uncle Sam on April 15, and how much you should pay in quarterly estimated taxes throughout the year. If your state has an income tax, you are also typically required to make estimated tax payments. Certain cities, such as New York City, also collect income tax as part of your state filing, so check with your accountant if your employer doesn't automatically withhold this tax for you.

For federal returns, you can find the address for filing your payments and due dates as part of Form 1040-ES. You may face a penalty if you didn't pay enough estimated tax for the year, or if you didn't make the payments on time or in the required amount. You can avoid the penalty as long as you pay at least 90 percent of the tax for the current year, or 100 percent of the tax you owed for the previous year, whichever is smaller.

Even with the precarious nature of a freelancer's finances, when you're disciplined and automate the withdrawals from your paychecks on a regular basis, you can avoid the springtime surprise of a steep tax bill and save for retirement one paycheck at a time. Think cruise control.

If you pay your taxes via electronic filing, for instance, you can schedule all four estimated future quarterly payments at once and save yourself the headache of potentially forgetting to mail a check.

One important caveat: When it comes to taxes, it's always an individual calculation. You should talk with a professional tax adviser to review your particular situation.

There are some potentially big savings for remote workers with business deductions. Here's a quick rundown of how the tax law could benefit those who work from home as freelancers or contractors.

Qualified business income deduction. Between now and 2025, many independent contractors may be entitled to lop off a tax deduction of 20 percent on qualified business income, providing you earn under certain preset amounts. Check with the IRS for current limitations. The details are complicated. It's intended to apply to "pass-through" business income for freelancers who have set their businesses up as partnerships, limited liability corporations, S corporations, or sole proprietorships. The nonpartisan Tax Policy Center provides a detailed analysis of the complex sweetener.

Standard deductions. The standard deduction is $12,200 for single filers and $24,400 for couples for 2020. The amount is set annually. If you're self-employed and fit the requirements, you can claim the standard deduction, plus the qualified business income deduction, and also deduct eligible business expenses such as rent, professional fees, training and education, licensing and certification fees, and supplies and travel costs.

Freelancers typically receive a form 1099-MISC, "Miscellaneous Income," from each client and report 1099 income—as well as expenses for home offices, travel, and supplies—on Schedule C, which is attached to form 1040. Here's a rundown of the six big tax deductions for expenses that freelancers may qualify for this year.

New equipment write-off. The tax law currently allows for the immediate expensing and a bonus depreciation percentage of 100 percent for qualified property acquired such as a new computer, software, office furniture, and even a car or truck, if the item was purchased and placed into service after September 27, 2017, and before January 1, 2023.

Business expenses. Deductible expenses can range from business meals and travel to gasoline for your car to postage and shipping to rent for the artist studio where you create jewelry or other crafts.

You can generally claim 50 percent of the cost of meals that you purchase for work purposes. Deductions claimed for client-entertainment costs (such as tickets to a sporting event or a concert) are not allowed. However, you typically can write off 50 percent of the cost for treating your client to a meal where you discuss business. Work-related travel expenses to meet with a client or attend a conference across town or across the country are 100 percent deductible.

Medical expenses. For most freelancers, health insurance and medical bills are a weighty part of your budget. You may deduct only the amount of your total medical expenses that exceed 7.5% of your adjusted gross income. You figure the amount you're allowed to deduct on Schedule A (Form 1040 or 1040-SR). If you bought your own health insurance policy, your medical expenses will also include insurance premiums. If you're self-employed and pay supplemental Medicare premiums, such as for Part B coverage, you can deduct these premiums.

Education and training. You can write off your costs for work-related education directly from your self-employment income as a business expense. These outlays include tuition, books, supplies, and transportation to and from classes, according to the IRS website. The expenses are deductible only if the education "maintains or improves skills needed in your present work." If you're going back to school to switch careers, you're out of luck. The lifetime learning credit, though, offers a tax credit of up to $2,000 to cover up to 20 percent of annual tuition, and you don't have to be enrolled in a degree program. (The benefit phases out at specific income levels that adjust annually. For more, see IRS Publication 970.)

Automobile expenses. You can deduct the number of miles you drive in your car for business, multiplied by the IRS's preset standard mileage rate of 57.5 cents per mile in 2020. This figure is reset annually. Keep a mileage log; you'll need it if you're audited. (Take a picture of your odometer at the beginning and the end of the year for backup documentation.) Your other option is to subtract your actual car expenses. These include depreciation, gas, oil, tolls, parking fees, insurance, lease payments, registration fees, repairs, and tires. For more, IRS Publication 463 provides details.

Your home office. If you work from your home or use part of it in your business, you should be able to deduct home-office expenses that are prorated, based on the size of your home and office. These are costs such as your mortgage or rent, insurance, and utility bills. If the square footage of your home office equals 10 percent of your home's total, you can claim 10 percent of its expenses. You might opt for the "simplified option" rule, which allows you to deduct $5 per square foot of your home office on your return, with a maximum write-off of $1,500 (based on a maximum of 300 square feet). You may want to take a picture of the space so that you have a record, in case the IRS does examine your return. To get the deduction, you must file form 8829, "Expenses for Business Use of Your Home," along with your Schedule C. You can read all the home-office rules in IRS Publication 587.

In general, to write off home-office outlays, you must use the "area" for work only and on a regular or constant basis, either as your primary place of business or as a setting to meet with clients or to do paperwork such as writing invoices, ordering supplies, and making phone calls. I suggest you snap a pic of the space, too, so you have a record in case the IRS is ever curious.

(As noted above: If you're a full-time employee at a business, you will only qualify for the deductions if the company doesn't provide you with an office within their workplace.)

Consider a Financial Management App

There are several money management apps designed to help you plan for taxes and retirement savings that you might want to investigate. Here's a look at a few of them.

Self-Saver (self-saver.org) offers a tax calculator, automated withholding on 1099 income, expense itemization, and quarterly filings to the IRS.

Qapital (qapital.com) is an app that allows you to move a percentage of a deposit from your bank account to an FDIC-insured account at a partner bank, where it is held by Qapital. You can take the money from the account and transfer it back to your checking account whenever you opt to do so.

The app, designed in partnership with Duke University behavioral economist Dan Ariely, lets you name a savings goal and then apply "rules" to help you get there, using funds from your linked bank account. For example, say your goal is to fund an IRA; your rule might be to divert 30 percent of any deposit you get above $1,000 to your selected savings account. Then you shift the funds to your IRA at a brokerage or fund company when you're ready. There is no fee to use the app.

Digit (digit.co) offers a smartphone app that connects to your checking account, analyzes spending habits, and every few days automatically sweeps a small amount of funds—typically between $5 and $50—into an FDIC-insured bank-level encrypted Digit savings account. Your funds can be shifted at any time to your personal checking account within one business day.

Intuit's QuickBooks Self-Employed (quickbooks.intuit.com/self-employed) tracks business expenses by scanning bank accounts and credit card transactions. It also calculates mileage and can be used to send invoices.

Expensify (use.expensify.com/self-employed) gathers expenses that need to be reimbursed, and you can create files to integrate with accounting software such as QuickBooks. The time-tracking can provide details of miles traveled and hours spent on a project.

Shoeboxed (shoeboxed.com) lets you scan and organize uploaded receipts under categories of reimbursable or deductible. The app uses a GPS signal to track your mileage when you leave your home office for a business appointment.

Do it yourself. You can also set up a comparable do-it-yourself automated process with your own bank. Each April, you can ask your accountant to tell you the amount you need for quarterly tax estimates based on the previous year's return. You divvy it up to sweep out a certain amount each month from your business checking account where your paychecks are deposited (usually electronically) and move it into a dedicated money market account. Not perfect, but at least it automates the process, and the funds are there when you need to tap them to pay quarterly estimates.

For retirement fund contributions, you likewise electronically sweep a preset amount of funds each month from your business checking account into a money market fund and make your annual contribution at tax time. You might also make regular contributions routinely to a retirement account you already hold and boost it at tax time, if you have the option.

NETWORKING FOR REMOTE WORKERS

In my books and columns, I often reach out to one of my go-to career coaches, Beverly Jones, author of *Think Like an Entrepreneur, Act Like a CEO* and host of the NPR-affiliated Jazzed About Work podcast.

"When you work *from* home it's tempting to stay *at* home, rarely leaving the comfort of your couch," says Jones. "But getting out and nurturing a strong network of in-person, real-life relationships is vital for your career—and for your best life. You probably know the critical importance of a broad network," she explains. "It helps you find customers and mentors, spot industry trends, and learn about new opportunities. And your connections are vital for any job search.

For *Great Pajama Jobs*, once again I have asked Jones to share her expertise. Following is her sage counsel:

"Surveys suggest that most successful job seekers tap their networks instead of simply relying on automated job sites. That's because hiring organizations prefer applicants with recommendations from a known source.

But the value of networking goes deeper than professional growth. Humans are inherently social. Our ancestors evolved with an understanding that we can't survive in isolation. Each of us has an inborn need to be connected with other people.

In recent years, the links between social connection and overall health and happiness have become clear. Experts say that people who have rewarding relationships, and who actually spend time with other folks, are more likely than their lonelier peers to build immunity, resilience, and good mental health. Connected people even live longer lives.

Aside from the studies, I know from clients and my own experience that if you're working remotely, it's particularly important to actively manage your social activity. You might think you won't miss hanging out daily with a work "family." But after the initial thrill of staying home all day, life may start to feel boring and lonely. And when you're by yourself for too long, it's harder to stay cheerful, maintain perspective, and generate fresh ideas."

Bev's Tips for nurturing a network with the power to support your career and enrich your life:

1. **Recognize that every person matters.** It's a mistake to think of your "network" as a long list of professional contacts. *Everyone* you know can impact your life, and often your more casual contacts are the ones most able to bring you opportunities.

    Try visualizing your network as a complex web of potentially helpful people, spreading out around you in concentric circles. The inner ring may include close friends and family. Further out are people you know only slightly, like alumni of your college, neighbors, and online connections. Think of ways to cultivate relationships in every ring.

2. **Start where you are.** "Networking" isn't just about forcing yourself to meet strangers. Perhaps more important is cultivating the contacts you already have. You can jumpstart your networking by reaching out to friends you seldom see. And you can start new friendships by chatting with folks in the places where you already hang out, like your gym, church, or local coffee shop.

3. **Use online platforms to locate people you know.** I'm assuming you know that online platforms are a great way to connect with potential employers and industry peers. But have you used their search features to reconnect with connections from past years? Particularly if they live nearby, you can turn former colleagues and acquaintances into new pals.

   Think of groups where you once hung out, from your childhood neighborhoods and college dorms to your former employers. Use LinkedIn or another app to identify people from those groups who now live close to you. Reconnect by sending messages. And when it feels right, suggest a coffee date.

4. **Practice "small talk."** You may avoid networking in person because you dislike the forced chitchat at the start of a social interaction. Maybe you feel awkward making inconsequential remarks like, "What a cold day!" Small talk sounds meaningless but the custom of exchanging trivial remarks plays a big role in helping people connect. Discussing trifling topics is a bonding ritual that can help build trust and rapport. If you struggle with chitchat, remind yourself that content doesn't matter. What counts most is friendly intent. Prepare for an encounter by thinking up a few noncontroversial discussion topics, like the local sports team or a recent movie. And build your small talk skill by practicing in places and events where you're most comfortable.

5. **Travel to meetings.** If you're invited to meet in person with your virtual teammates or distant clients, do try to attend. Even if the meeting agenda doesn't justify the trip, the benefits of face-to-face conversation can be priceless. When you are actually in the presence of someone you can use the full scope of your relationship-building skills. You can forge a deeper connection by listening intently, expressing empathy and humor, and perhaps sharing a meal.

6. **Consider co-working spaces.** Even if you love working in your home office, there are benefits to varying your routine. Many communities have inexpensive co-working facilities where you might enjoy working some days. Shared spaces may offer resources like commercial-grade equipment and Wi-Fi. More important, they give you a chance to connect with the local remote worker community. You might meet potential colleagues, partners, mentors, and entertaining lunch buddies.

7. **Widen your circles.** People who stick with colleagues in the same profession or locale risk developing "closed" networks. That means they mostly bump into people with similar interests, backgrounds, and worldviews. A closed network can bring you support, but you get so much more from an "open" network that includes a wide variety of people.

When you move within diverse communities you have endless chances to expand your knowledge, spot emerging trends, and find unexpected opportunities. Scientists who study human connection patterns suggest that an "open," varied network is a key predictor of career success. So as you consider possible networking opportunities, don't limit yourself to the most obvious. Look for options that push you a bit out of your comfort zone and hold the promise of introducing you to a new crowd.

8. **Pursue hobbies.** Studies suggest you'll be more productive at work if you devote some of your life to leisure activities. When you pursue your favorite pastimes, you're more relaxed and better at problem solving and collaborating once you're back on the job. And a fun way to meet people from outside your professional track is to find groups and activities built around your hobbies. Meetup.com is one helpful platform for finding people who share your interests. When you search there, choose a category like "Arts," "Photography," or "Food and Drink," then look for activities or organizations near you.

9. **Get moving in groups.** Research reveals that not only are we hardwired to connect with other people, but we are also created to enjoy frequent physical movement. Becoming too sedentary can threaten our health, our mood, our ability to solve problems, and our creativity.

Try socializing at the same time you exercise by joining a group or class. As fitness companies like CrossFit have found, a special kind of bonding occurs when people exercise together. Apps like Meetup and Eventbrite can help you find local groups who build community as they dance, hike, do yoga, walk dogs, climb rocks, or paddle canoes.

10. **Volunteer.** Sometimes the world feels like a mess. But here's some good networking news: One of the best ways to build connections is by volunteering for a cause or project you care about. Studies say that volunteers typically make new friends and create more meaning in their lives. An excellent way to expand your circle is to volunteer with a nonprofit group, then gradually work your way to membership on a committee or board.

You are a social creature with a deep need to stay connected. Having a varied web of relationships is good for your health and can bring you confidence, positive energy, and a sense of well-being. The inevitable flow of professional opportunities generated by a vibrant network is only one of many reasons why remote workers should get out of the house and regularly connect with the world.

193

Afterword

F inding success as a remote worker takes get-up-and-go. It requires a balancing act, motivation, and—yep, I will harp on it once again— self-discipline.

I *love* working remotely. As I write these final words, it's nearly 5 p.m., and yes, I'm still in my comfy PJs, sweatshirt, and soft socks. I'm madly typing away, lost in my writer's zone. Zena, my Labrador retriever, is curled up alongside me, oblivious to my intensity. I'm grateful for the calm aura she exudes. In fact, many of the happy campers I interviewed for this book who work from home told me that having their pets with them during their working hours brought them a joy that's tough to quantify, but is a centering force.

I'm perched in a comfy spot on the porch of a modest cottage overlooking a glistening pond, a herd of horses, and the blue-toned Shenandoah Mountains in the distance.

Not a bad place to work. My commute is less than 10 seconds.

That said, regardless of your age or career stage (or whether you have a pet at home), remote working packs a psychological boost that comes from savoring autonomy and flexibility.

Technology has profoundly transformed how—and where—we work. And for many of us, working from home is also a financial gain. It's cost-effective–a bona fide savings of time from jettisoning the commute and office distractions, as well as a savings of money spent on transportation and meals out.

It didn't surprise me that a study by Princeton University economics professor Alexandre Mas and Harvard economics professor Amanda Pallais found job applicants were willing to accept 8 percent less pay for the option to work from home. But, of course, as you've gleaned from this guide to great pajama jobs, a pay cut isn't a prerequisite at all.

Importantly, for those of us who embrace this way of working, it has made it far easier to make each day truly count. We've learned how to work efficiently so that we're able to create room in our lives for our families and friends, caregiving, hobbies, exercise, and more.

My hope is that you leave these pages with a plate rich with remote job possibilities to consider, a solid list of companies that value remote workers for you to explore, and the tools not only to land a remote job opportunity, but to make it a winning one for you personally and professionally.

Remote working is not about working less. No slackers need apply. It is about valuing ourselves, our talents, our independence, and our lives.

And that's precisely the ticket to falling in love with a *great* pajama job. You're fully engaged, enthusiastic, and productive. You're making a difference with the work you do, contributing your intrinsic skills to an organization's mission and genuinely touching the lives of others, whether it's through a product you're tasked with creating, or a service you deliver. A *great* pajama job frees you to do your best work ever. You've got this.

My goal is to help you succeed as a remote worker. Of course, we all have different work styles and setups, but as I wrap up this book, I will leave you with my best list of reminders.

Keep a regular work schedule. Take control of your time, so you are not working more hours than ever. Trust me, you will do your best work if you follow your own rhythm and know when to step away for your mental and physical well-being.

Put firm boundaries in place. I harp on this one throughout this book. Red light warning: This one is easy to disregard, and it will come back to haunt you. You have to be careful that co-workers, managers, friends, and family don't take advantage of your personal and work time. It can be an intrusion on one or the other, depending on who it is.

Seriously, get out of your pj's. I know this book is called *Great Pajama Jobs,* and you might linger in your pajamas longer than you would if you had to grab the train to work. But I find I am more in a work mindset when I at least pull on a clean pair of jeans or pants I would happily wear in office setting, and a turtleneck or tidy top, and I suspect you will, too. Of course, if you have a video conference scheduled, spruce it up, pronto.

Be comfortable with tech tools. Whether it is Slack messaging or Zoom, Skype, or FaceTime video meetings, it has to be a seamless communication for you. Use organization or time management tools if they help. These include Evernote, Microsoft Teams, Trello, Google Docs, Workplace from Facebook, and Asana.

Have a smart office setup. I know I didn't dig into this topic in the book for space reasons, but this is important. Make sure you have an ergonomic chair and desk setup so that your computer monitor and keypad don't cause any unnecessary strain on your back, eyes, wrists, and so on. You don't need to add on any physical stress.

Don't forget to eat with an eye to nutrition. I start each morning at 5:30 a.m. with a mug of black coffee, but 8 a.m. is breakfast time without fail. I make sure I have yogurt or oatmeal and a banana. And I take a lunch break, too.

It's important not to skip meals to keep your brain and body energy humming. It's super easy to forget to stop to eat properly, or to simply snack all day when you don't have a co-worker suggesting you run out to grab a bite or go down to the cafeteria. I keep a bag of mandarin oranges in the fridge for snacking and always have bananas on hand.

Stop and take a breather. Step outside. Pick up a magazine article to read that you've set aside, or a book—something not on your computer screen, to rest your eyes. Call your mom. Sip a cup of tea on your porch. Walk your dog. Whatever it is that helps you pause and recharge, do it. I like to take a break every few hours and stretch, but you will figure out what works for you. These breaks are essential to your wellness.

Talk to your boss and co-workers. Try to set daily meetings with your manager so you're on the same page and check in with co-workers, so you don't miss out on office happenings.

Before you shut down for the day, write your to-do action plan for the next day. The best way to hit the ground running each morning is to prepare ahead of time.

My parting thought for you is from my favorite Irish blessing:

May the road rise up to meet you. May the wind be always at your back. May the sun shine warm upon your face, and rains fall soft upon your fields. . .until we meet again.

Index

Gen Zers (*Continued*)
  independent contractor rates among, 186
  Workforce Institute's survey on flexibility and, 16
George Kaiser Family Foundation, 10
GitLab, 8
Glassdoor.com
  on digital marketing/social media specialist/manager salary range, 39
  job board of, 134
  learn about prospective employer using, 146
  principal biostatistician, 61
  on web search evaluator/search marketing specialist salary range, 44
Global Workplace Analytics, 3
Goettle, April, 11–12
Google
  Google+, 29
  Google certification, 106
  Google chats, 125
  Google Docs, 121, 128, 197
  identifying scams by searching on, 113–114
  IT Professional Support Certificate program of, 164
  programs specifically for military spouses, 164
Gotomeeting, 125
Grant/proposal writers, 28–29
Grants analyst (PRA Health Sciences), 94
Grant Writing for Dummies, 29

Graphic designers
  information about working as, 22–23
  Salesforce's position on, 102
Gray & Christmas, Inc., 3
Great Resumes Fast, 144
Green Building Certification Institute, 68

H
Hairdressers, 31
"Happy place" visualization, 182
Hard skills
  description of desirable, 129–130
  examining your, 133–134
  redeploying your, 134
Harshbarger, Brandon, 111–112
The Hartford, 63
Harvard University, 195
HCA Healthcare, 94
Healthcare/medical jobs
  Aetna's case manager, 89
  Aetna's senior analyst, 89–90
  BroadPath Healthcare Solutions' credentialing specialist, 87
  CVS Health positions, 102–103
  dietician and nutritionist, 54–55
  Fertility utilization review RN (UnitedHealth Group), 81
  healthcare/patient advocate, 58–59
  as hottest field for remote workers, 54
  Humana's medical director, 85
  massage therapist, 55–56
  medical biller/coder, 56–57
  medical interpreter, 57–58
  medical proofreader, 76–77
  medical records transcriptionist, 65, 96

for veterans and military spouses, 164–167

where to find remote jobs by, 134–136

writing a résumé and cover letter for, 137–148

See also Companies

PTIN (Preparer Tax Identification Number), 136

Publicists/public relations specialists, 27–28

Public relations jobs

marketing/communications associate or manager, 29

publicists/public relations specialists, 27–28

Public Relations Society of America (PRSA), 29

Public speaking courses, 151

Punctuality, 154

Q

Qapital app, 189

Qualified business income deduction, 187

Quality assurance specialists, 42

Quality controller (Lionbridge), 72

Quarterly taxes payments, 17, 179, 185, 190

QuickBooks

accountant and auditors, 34

bookkeeper skills with, 32

financial manager skills with, 33

QuickBooks Self-Employed app, 190

R

Rat Race Rebellion, 8, 112

Ratracerebellion.com, 135

Ratzlaff, Jim, 47–48

Recruiters

flagging those on LinkedIn, 24

Kelly Services, 76

Motion Recruitment Partners, 90–91

as popular job with military spouses, 162

Reliability, 133

Remote coaches, 124

Remote.co, 2, 8, 112, 135

Remote job post example, 136

Remote jobs

conventional professional type of, 16–17

FlexJobs' analysis on increasing rates of, 17

FlexJobs research identifying "remote-friendly" jobs, 69–70

freelance/contractor type of, 17

general tips on getting, 6–9

leading companies regularly hiring for, 7–8

Millennials' preferred five top locations for, 176–179

sources for finding valid, 112

twelve tips for working from home, 179–183

See also Jobs

Remote job search

developing/promoting technical skills, 127–128

example of a remote job post, 136

general tips on getting jobs, 6–9

highlight your telecommuting experience, 127

identifying skills remote employers value, 128–134

interviews, 149–159